ACCESSIBLE
TRAILS IN
WASHINGTON'S
BACKCOUNTRY

D0187966

ACCESSIBLE
TRAILS IN WASHINGTON'S BACKCOUNTRY

A GUIDE TO
85
OUTINGS

The Washington Trails Association

Edited by Dan A. Nelson

THE
MOUNTAINEERS

Published by
The Mountaineers
1001 SW Klickitat Way, Suite 102
Seattle, Washington 98134

© 1995 by Washington Trails Association

All rights reserved

9 8 7 6 5
5 4 3 2 1

No part of this book may be reproduced in any form, or by any electronic, mechanical, or other means, without permission in writing from the publisher.

Published simultaneously in Canada by Douglas & McIntyre, Ltd., 1615 Venables Street, Vancouver, B.C. V5L 2H1

Published simultaneously in Great Britain by Cordee, 3a DeMontfort Street, Leicester, England, LE1 7HD

Manufactured in the United States of America

Edited by Sherri Schultz
Maps by Partners in Design
All photographs by Bob and Ira Spring except as noted
Cover design by The Mountaineers Books
Book design and typography by The Mountaineers Books
Layout by Gray Mouse Graphics

Cover photograph: *Picture Lake and Mt. Shuksan* (Dale Strouse)
Frontispiece: *Hoodoo Peak from Blackpine Lake* (Photo: USFS, Methow Valley
    Ranger District)

Library of Congress Cataloging–in–Publication Data

Accessible trails in Washington's backcountry : a guide to 85 outings /
    the Washington Trails Association ; edited by Dan A. Nelson.
        p.   cm.
    Includes index.
    ISBN 0-89886-439-9
    1. Hiking—Washington (State)—Guidebooks.   2. Trails—Access for the
physically handicapped—Washington (State)   3. Handicapped—Travel—
Washington (State)—Guidebooks.   I. Nelson, Dan A.   II. Washington
Trails Association.
GV199.42.W22A33   1995
796.5'1'09797—dc20   95–11184
                                                               CIP

♻ Printed on recycled paper

CONTENTS

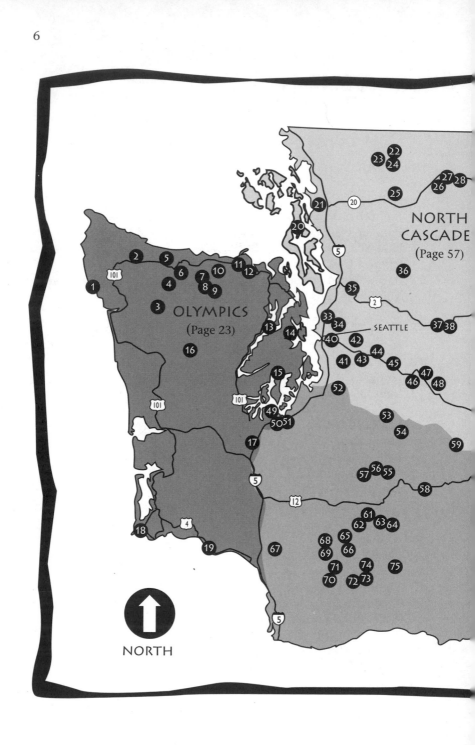

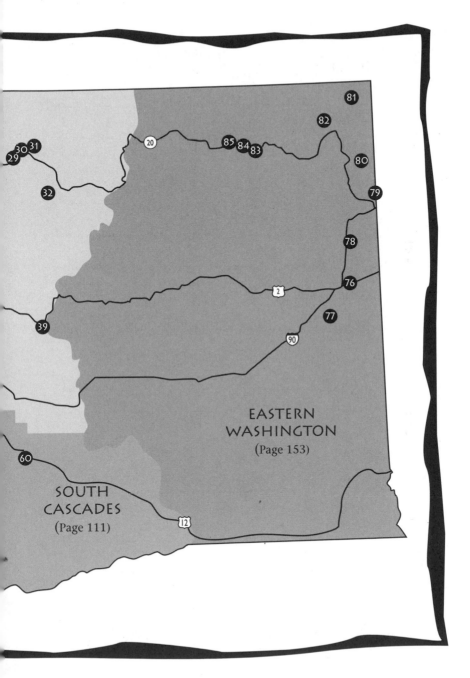

EASTERN
WASHINGTON
(Page 153)

SOUTH
CASCADES
(Page 111)

Rainy Lake (Trail no. 20)

FOREWORD

I love the outdoors. But for me and millions of other Americans with disabilities, the available choices for outdoor recreation have been unnecessarily limited.

In the past, facilities have been designed for the "average person." And often these designs excluded those of us with disabilities. Yet, thanks to a series of federal laws, more and more facilities are being made accessible.

In 1920, Congress passed the first federal laws in support of people with disabilities. This was a response to the widespread needs of veterans injured in World War I. A few decades later, people with disabilities benefited from advances in medicine and rehabilitation.

In 1959, a presidential advisory committee published guidelines on barrier-free design. Federal architecture standards were established to ensure that people with disabilities had access to federal buildings.

In 1990, Congress passed the Americans with Disabilities Act (ADA), which improved access for everyone. It set new standards for access to private as well as government facilities.

While there has been progress in making urban settings universally accessible, until recently there were few places where I could enjoy the wilderness. Fortunately, that's changing. The U.S. Forest Service has been a leader in addressing outdoor-recreation accessibility issues. The Forest Service's design guide focuses on universal design, a new approach that considers the needs of all users—including children, the elderly, and people with mobility, sensory, cognitive, and temporary disabilities. These designs foster a sense of dignity and independence for all visitors. We don't want "handicapped trails." We want outdoor recreation for everyone.

Today, I see more people with disabilities taking pleasure in the extraordinary challenges of outdoor recreation. Technological developments have fueled our drive for outdoor independence. Thirty years ago a wheelchair weighed fifty-five pounds. Today, my mountain wheelchair weighs twenty-six pounds, and I can take on far more rugged terrain than ever before. With well-designed equipment, disabled people can now enjoy bicycling, cross-country skiing, marathons, and even rock climbing.

But providing barrier-free trails is not enough. People must know about them and be encouraged to use them. The volunteers at Washington Trails Association (WTA) have made a crucial contribution to accessible outdoor recreation in Washington state. The significance of their work researching, writing, and developing a partnership with the Forest Service and other government agencies cannot be overemphasized. Just the act of writing this book has focused new attention on maintaining existing trails and building new ones. (WTA's work crews have also spent over 500 volunteer hours building and maintaining barrier-free trails throughout the state.)

I hope you enjoy these trails as much as I have. See you on the trail!

Chuck Frayer, Accessibility Specialist
U.S. Forest Service

PREFACE

There truly are trails for all Americans.

Many Americans long to enjoy the vast array of wilderness experiences offered by this beautiful state, but are physically unable to utilize the rough-and-tumble mountain trails that are most commonly found in our wild areas. While Washingtonians routinely rate hiking as their number one outdoor activity, a large segment of the population is unable to get out on the average hiking trail: census studies show that one in ten Americans is temporarily disabled at any one time, and nearly one in three Americans over age 65 has some form of disability. Considering that when a family member's mobility is limited, the entire family is affected, that is a lot of outdoor enthusiasts who are able to enjoy only fully accessible trails.

Those of us who have worked on trails issues in Washington know that this state boasts an assortment of fully accessible trails, some in the most beautiful, scenic sections of the wilderness. At the same time, we realize that these trails are virtually unknown to the population that would enjoy them the most: the young and the old, the physically challenged, the visually impaired, and anyone seeking a gentle trail in a natural environment.

Prior to this book, few—if any—trail guidebooks mentioned barrier-free trails, and certainly none were written solely about these fully accessible routes. Yet dozens of guidebooks have been written about the wide network of other wilderness trails in Washington. Climbers, hikers, horse riders, and mountain bikers have been able to use these reference books to find enjoyable trail experiences. Our goal with *Accessible Trails in Washington's Backcountry* is to fill this gap in wilderness trail guidebooks. We hope to help bring a wilderness experience to anyone and everyone who wants one.

With that in mind, a hardworking team of Washington Trails

Association volunteers spent more than two years researching all the barrier-free trails in Washington and culling the best 85 from the list. These top trails are described in this book. All of the trails were visited and traveled at least once by members of the research team to assure accurate descriptions. This extensive field work meant hundreds of hours spent driving and researching. The members of our research team volunteered their time and money simply because they saw a need for a guide that would help spread the enjoyment of the outdoors to everyone who wants to share in it.

I want to thank the more than thirty-five people who helped make this book possible, both the core members of the team—Greg and Susan Ball, Julie Wysocki, Michelle Conner, Lisa Robinson, Mary Masterson, Margaret Schuler, Susan Anderson, Glenna Lynch, and Darcy Heiber—and the score of others who assisted them. Their long hours of work made the task of writing and editing much easier. This book truly is a result of their hard work and dedication.

Dan A. Nelson

INTRODUCTION

Washington is a unique state with a vast array of wild regions, offering recreational experiences in virtually every ecosystem found in North America, from high mountains to deep canyons, deserts to ocean beaches, inland seas to winding rivers and streams.

For most of the twentieth century, hiking trails have pierced each of these ecosystems, and hikers have explored and enjoyed them all. But only recently, in the past several decades, have Washington's unique wild environments been made accessible to all the state's residents and visitors.

Today, trails are open and accessible for all outdoor enthusiasts regardless of their size, physical strength, or means of mobility. Everyone can enjoy trails that weave through high, alpine flower meadows; trails that loop around cold, clear mountain lakes; trails that wind through sagebrush and jackrabbit-filled deserts.

This book is designed to help bring these barrier-free, fully accessible trails to any and all outdoor enthusiasts who long to taste the wind, see the rugged beauty, and feel the wild spirit of our wildest environs.

ABOUT THE TRAILS

Washington Trails Association's team of researchers visited all accessible, barrier-free trails on public land in Washington and evaluated them. We selected the best 85 barrier-free trails in Washington state, offering a variety of easy to difficult terrain, for inclusion in this guide. These top trails either have an outstanding feature or attraction, such as waterfalls or wildlife viewing opportunities, or are simply exceptionally nice trails. Generally, these trails are found in or near the backcountry and offer wilderness-like settings. Some of these trails are in such spectacular areas that the drive to the

trailhead itself makes a nice outing. Because of time and space con-
straints, many of the more well-known but less scenic urban trails
were omitted from this book.

This guidebook was developed with one goal in mind—to bring
the joy of the wilderness to everyone who wants to experience it.
Toward that end, it is designed to provide details on each trail's level
of accessibility as well as descriptions of the local environments and
scenery found along each trail.

To further help you select trails to explore and enjoy, this book
divides the state into four regions: the North Cascades, the South
Cascades, the Olympics, and Eastern Washington. The trails are
listed by region; within each region, the trails are listed in map order
as you read the map from left to right and top to bottom.

DESCRIPTIONS AND
INFORMATION BLOCKS

This book also rates the trails on their accessibility. Since most of
the trails are in national forests, we have adopted the Forest Service's
categories for trails: easy, moderate, and difficult. (These standards
have not yet been accepted into law and are not the same as those
developed for the Americans with Disabilities Act.) We formulated
our ratings with the manual wheelchair user in mind. For users of
other types of equipment, such as power wheelchairs or three-
wheeled scooters, the trail difficulty may vary. For example, a trail
with a "moderate" access rating may seem "easy" to a power wheelchair user. However, a trail with a "difficult" access rating may be
impossible for a power wheelchair user, because this type of trail
often involves rugged terrain or the ability to do "wheelies." If a
trail has a short section of difficult terrain, we rate the whole trail
as difficult, and also note in the trail description whether the section could be accomplished with a little assistance. As in any other
type of outdoor situation, please consider your type of equipment
and your abilities when approaching a new trail.

At the beginning of each trail description you'll find a small information block. The information in these blocks is included to help
you find trails that suit your abilities and desires.

Accessibility: The following criteria were used in rating each trail.

E   *Easy*—urban/rural. These trails are paved and have gentle slopes.
Fishing and scenic overlooks include handrails. The minimum

trail width is 48 inches. A maximum 5 percent grade is allowed for a maximum distance of 50 feet.

M *Moderate*—roaded/natural. These trails may be leveled with compact gravel rather than paved, and may have slightly steeper slopes. Handrails at fishing sites may be replaced by barriers constructed of natural materials, such as boulders or logs, in order to allow angling opportunities for all. The minimum trail width is 36 inches. A maximum 5 to 8 percent grade is allowed for a maximum distance of 50 feet.

D *Difficult*—semiprimitive. These are often simply dirt trails and are narrower and steeper. They tend to offer less accessible features but more of a "wilderness" experience. The minimum trail width is 28 inches. A maximum 12 percent grade is allowed for a maximum distance of 30 feet.

Distances: All trail distances described in this book are round trip. While most of the trails are relatively short loop routes, there are also some longer routes that may be broken into smaller sections by using various combinations of alternative trailheads and shorter link trails (not all trails have both options—see the specific trail descriptions for individual trails).

Gradient: This is the highest degree of incline found on the trail. The gradient was also used in determining the accessibility rating, but it can be an important consideration on its own, especially for those in muscle-powered wheelchairs.

Surface: This describes the material used to harden the surface of the trail. Usually it is hardened dirt, compacted gravel, or asphalt.

When to go: This is merely a recommendation based on typical weather conditions, flower blooming cycles, and other variables. The best times to visit will vary slightly from year to year, but this is a general guideline.

   🌷 *Spring*—March through May

   ☀️ *Summer*—June through August

   🍁 *Autumn*—September through November

   ❄️ *Winter*—December through February

Parking: While parking is available at all the trailheads, not all trails feature designated handicapped parking spaces. Therefore, parking is rated either "usable" or "designated" to distinguish between the two kinds of parking areas. At popular trailheads where there is no designated parking, users may have to navigate crowded parking lots to get to the trailhead. Also, there are a few trails that have no parking of any kind at the trailhead. In these cases, the best approach is to take along an assistant. That person can then drop you off at the trailhead before parking the vehicle.

Restrooms: Not all trails feature restroom facilities, and some that do lack fully accessible facilities. In the information block, "yes" means that accessible restrooms are provided, while "no" means that the restrooms, if any, are not accessible.

Information: This is the name and telephone number of the agency that manages and maintains the trail. It is the place to call for more information, such as current road and trail conditions.

MAPS

The maps in this book are designed to show you where the trails are located relative to each other and to the geographic features of the state. Feel free to use the maps to plan your trips. Some trails are close enough to each other that you will be able to explore more than one in a day.

These maps, however, are not detailed enough to assist you in plotting your exact route to and from the trails. Please use a current road map to help you navigate to the trailheads. The trail descriptions include directions to the trails, but these are sometimes easier to understand if you have a detailed road map in front of you.

Like the text, the maps group the trails into four regions: the North Cascades, the South Cascades, the Olympics, and Eastern Washington.

YOUR TRAIL ADVENTURES

The beauty of these trails is what makes venturing along them such a joy, and it is the responsibility of each and every trail user to keep them beautiful. Fortunately, that is relatively easy to do. By simply staying on the trails, you accomplish much. The trails listed here are generally hard packed or paved and can bear a lot of traffic, but the surrounding meadows, forests, and wetlands are fragile; even one set of tracks through a wildflower meadow can leave an indelible mark on the land.

Similarly, a wildflower in a meadow can be seen and enjoyed by thousands, but when picked and carried away, it quickly shrivels and dies, so not even the picker can enjoy it. Gather souvenirs and keepsakes with your camera, not your clippers.

It is also vital to the health and beauty of the trail environment that visitors carry out any garbage they bring with them. Things such as soda cans and candy wrappers detract from the wilderness setting and take decades to degrade and disappear. In fact, conscientious trail users will pick up any litter they see along the route. leaving the trail cleaner than they found it.

PREPARING FOR A TRIP

This guide has been organized in a user-friendly format, with as much trail information as possible, to make selecting and getting to a trail easy. It is highly recommended, however, that you take the time to get extra information before venturing out on any of these trails. Road, trail, and weather conditions can change quickly, and the only way to get the best, most current information is to call the people in charge of the trails.

At the beginning of each trail description, we have listed the phone number of the agency that manages the trail, so you can call before you begin your trip. This way you can avoid taking a long drive only to find the trail closed. Backcountry trails are more difficult to maintain than are "frontcountry" (urban) trails because they are more subject to the whims of nature. Especially in the early spring, trees knocked down by winter storms may obstruct trails, making them impassable to hikers with disabilities. The land managers try to send out trail crews as soon as possible, but often it takes some time to remove the obstructions.

Because these are backcountry trails, it is important that you be adequately prepared for your adventure. Weather conditions can change quickly in the mountains, and unexpected trail conditions can force a longer stay than you had planned. Therefore, always carry the following items, even on what appears to be a short trail: extra clothing (windproof, rain-repellent poncho and warm clothing of wool or synthetic fabrics, but not cotton), extra food, sunglasses, insect repellent, knife, fire starter, first-aid kit, matches in a waterproof container, flashlight, map, and compass.

One final piece of emergency gear that is becoming more common in the backcountry is a cellular telephone. If you have access to one of these high-tech phones, you may want to toss it in your pack. More and more wilderness rescues are having happy endings simply because the person in need of aid was able to call for help quickly.

Here are some other things you may want to carry along just to make your adventure more enjoyable: camera (video or still), notebook and pencil, wildflower or bird identification field guides, binoculars, and a companion with whom you can share your experiences.

APPENDICES

The first appendix consists of a comprehensive chart listing each of the trails included in this book. The trails and their features— accessibility rating, distance, trail surface, and region—are listed side by side for easy comparisons.

Another appendix lists some trails that were planned but not yet constructed when this book was published. By the time you read this, these trails may be open. Call the trail manager listed for each trail to get the latest information.

THE FUTURE OF BARRIER-FREE TRAILS

Several new barrier-free trails are in the planning and construction stages; however, we have described only existing trails in this guide. The appendices contain a list of additional barrier-free trails currently being constructed or considered for the future.

A surprising number of trails and experiences are already accessible to all. However, Washington Trails Association sees the need for land managers (the U.S. Forest Service, the state parks, the National Park Service) to plan and coordinate as a group rather than as single agencies. Too many of the available trails are simply short nature trails through old-growth forests. We would like the agencies to redirect their focus toward a larger variety of trails. Routes to waterfalls, paths along streams and lakes, and trails into high-country meadows are a few of the experiences that should be more plentiful for all users.

Accessible trails are beginning to suffer from the same lack of maintenance money that has plagued the state's trail system for years. Accessible trails need more maintenance than the normal foot trail. Grass growing between the gravel base, downed trees, and overgrown bushes that encroach upon the trail—these kinds of maintenance problems could close a trail to wheelchair users, while the hiker with more mobility might not even notice them.

We welcome your comments on this book. Maybe you know about a great trail that should be added. Or perhaps the conditions of a trail we describe have changed since the book was published. Please send us any comments or information that you feel would improve this book. You will find our address and telephone number at the end of this book.

A NOTE ABOUT SAFETY

Safety is an important concern in all outdoor activities. No guidebook can alert you to every hazard or anticipate the limitations of every reader. Therefore, the descriptions of roads, trails, routes, and natural features in this book are not representations that a particular place or excursion will be safe for your party. When you follow any of the routes described in this book, you assume responsibility for your own safety. Under normal conditions, such excursions require the usual attention to traffic, road and trail conditions, weather, terrain, the capabilities of your party, and other factors. Keeping informed on current conditions and exercising common sense are the keys to a safe, enjoyable outing.

The Mountaineers

OLYMPICS

1
RIALTO BEACH

E 🌱 ☀️ 🍂 ❄️

Accessibility:	Easy
Distance:	0.1 mile round trip
Gradient:	Generally flat, with 5% grade to view spot
Surface:	Pavement
When to go:	All year
Parking:	Designated
Restrooms:	Yes
Information:	Olympic National Park, (360) 452-4501

For those seeking a beach experience that doesn't require dodging ice chests and kite lines, the wilderness beaches of Washington offer the chance to experience the Pacific Coast as it was 200 years ago. This trail on Rialto Beach, located in the Mora Beach Area, is indisputably one of the most beautiful beaches in the area.

From Forks, drive north on US Highway 101 to the La Push and Mora Beach turnoff. Turn west and continue along this route, following signs toward Mora Beach. The Rialto Beach Trail is found before reaching Mora and is well marked, so watch for the signs.

This accessible trail begins at the parking area and travels 0.1 mile through coastal forest to a platform on the beach. The first things to capture your attention are the surf and the surf-sculpted rock formations, but as you watch the water, keep an eye out for other area visitors—harbor seals, sea lions, and gray whales. Taking a closer look on shore, notice the gnarled beauty of driftwood stacked on the beach by winter storms, and enjoy the smell of the salt air on the ever-present breeze. Bring a coat: even on sunny days, the winds can be chilly.

The accessibility of the platform depends on the amount of driftwood and cobblestones that have washed onto it at the time of your visit. At the end of the platform, you can see many islands in the distance. All, with the exception of James Island, are part of the Washington Island National Wildlife Refuge. We rated this trail easy

Hurricane Ridge Lodge and Mount Carrie (Trail no. 9)

OLYMPICS

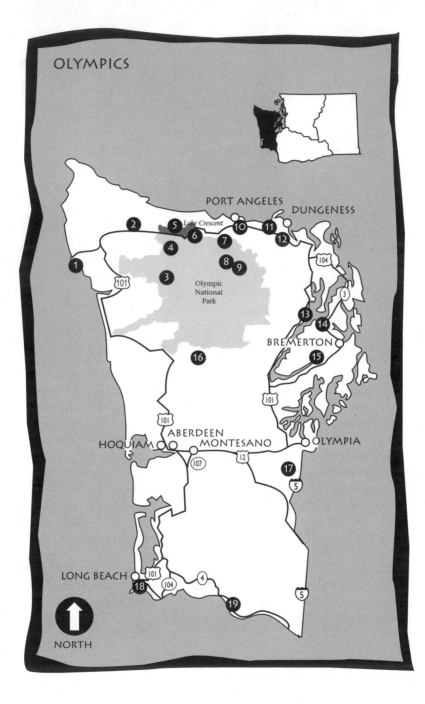

PORT ANGELES   DUNGENESS

Lake Crescent

Olympic
National
Park

BREMERTON

ABERDEEN
HOQUIAM   MONTESANO   OLYMPIA

LONG BEACH

NORTH

Looking north from Rialto Beach

to access, with its gradient a minimal 1 percent, except for a 5 percent grade to the elevated platform.

   Roughly halfway down the trail is an accessible picnic area that
includes a picnic table with no bench on one side.

2
PIONEER TRAIL

M 🌱 ☀ 🍂 ❄

Accessibility:	Moderate
Distance:	0.25 mile loop
Gradient:	To 8%
Surface:	Gravel
When to go:	All year, when dry enough
Parking:	Usable
Restrooms:	Yes (in campground)
Information:	USFS Sol Duc District, (360) 374-6522

This trail follows a portion of the area's original trade route, which later became a main U.S. Forest Service access trail. Entering the dark, mossy forest on the downhill grade, you hear the Sol Duc River in the distance. As you meander through the thick underbrush of salal, huckleberry, and sword fern, you dodge stumps, fallen trees, and nurse logs. The air is rich with the smell of bark and foliage, and as you approach the river, vine maples and other deciduous trees let light fleck the forest carpet.

As you climb the gradual hill, take time to pause at the river overlook. High on the bank, you can study the water and beautiful stones; the sounds here are especially refreshing. Returning to the hill, you encounter the steepest portion of trail. The trail is graveled to this point, but the grade is still steep.

The trail from here on lacks gravel, but it is wide and barrier-free, with many turnouts for resting and viewing the intricacies of your surroundings. Be careful if the weather has been damp; the gravel-less portion of trail can be extremely muddy. On top of the hill you reenter the deep forest. Here the nurse logs are astounding, the undergrowth delicate, and the vine maples draped with moss.

From Port Angeles, follow US Highway 101 west about 9 miles past the end of Lake Crescent; then turn into the Klahowya Campground on the right (north) side of the highway. Follow the one-way loop through the main campground. The trailhead is located near the far end of the loop.

3
HOH MINI-LOOP NATURE TRAIL

Accessibility: Easy
Distance: 0.25 mile loop
Gradient: From 1% to 4%
Surface: Pavement
When to go: June–October, when dry
Parking: Designated
Restrooms: Yes
Information: Olympic National Park, (360) 452-4501

Though it is called a mini-trail, this loop is packed with stunningly beautiful scenery.

Starting at the Hoh Rain Forest Visitor Center, the trail is a 0.25-mile loop through an old-growth rain forest—the type of forest that graces postcards and book covers.

The moss, ferns, lichens, twisting branches, and eerie shadows can make this a truly surreal experience. The preferred time to visit is mid-spring, when the multitude of plants all push out new growth in vibrant colors—or, more accurately, in vibrant *color*. Green seems to be the only color around, but there so many different shades of green that you won't care about the dearth of other colors.

The Olympic rain forests owe their unique qualities—and the ecology of this area is like that of no other place in the world—to the weather. These river valleys on the western slope of the Olympic Mountains receive an average of 142 inches of rain per year (compared with Seattle's 32 inches per year). Also, the low elevation and coastal winds combine to keep the temperatures moderate year-round.

Given the special nature of this area, don't be surprised if you feel that you've entered a long-lost enchanted forest. Moss-laden trees—fir, cedar, and hemlock mingle with big-leaf and vine maples—are everywhere, and you will feel dwarfed by the massive roots of these ancient giants. Notice, too, that even in death, the

Hoh Rain Forest near the Visitor Center

big trees provide new life to the forest. Nurse logs cover the ground, offering their rotten trunks to the roots of new, young trees. This trail is definitely a must-see!

From Forks, drive south on US Highway 101 and watch for the Hoh Rain Forest turnoff just past the town limits. Turn east and proceed into the Olympic National Park until you reach the Hoh Visitor Center, the hub for all the area trailheads.

4
SALMON CASCADES

Accessibility:	Easy
Distance:	0.1 mile round trip
Gradient:	From 3% to 5%
Surface:	Gravel
When to go:	All year
Parking:	Designated
Restrooms:	Yes
Information:	Olympic National Park, (360) 452-4501

Located on Sol Duc Hot Springs Road, this short trail offers a wonderful wilderness experience to enjoy before immersing yourself in the steaming pleasures of the hot springs. The gravel trail leads

Salmon leaping the Salmon Cascades on the Sol Duc River

through a lush forest to a rustic wooden platform overlooking the Sol Duc River. The water has a hypnotic effect on most visitors, luring them into long, silent contemplation of the roiling river and the lush, green moss on the banks. During the fall, spawning salmon crowd the shallows and fight for position as they are pulled upstream by their primal instincts.

To get to the trailhead, follow US Highway 101 just west of Lake Crescent to the Sol Duc Hot Springs sign. Turn south and continue about 7 miles. The parking area and trailhead are on the right.

5

BARNES POINT NATURE TRAIL

Accessibility: Moderate
Distance: 1 mile round trip
Gradient: Flat
Surface: Compacted gravel
When to go: All year
Parking: Usable
Restrooms: Yes
Information: Olympic National Park, (360) 452-4501

Built entirely by volunteers, this trail explores the natural as well as the human history of the Olympic Peninsula.

Huge old-growth trees tower over the lush, green forest floor. Proving the incredible age of this ancient forest are the rotten hulks of centuries-old trees that likely lived and died before our nation was born. From these decaying logs grows the new generation of forest; thus they are referred to as nurse logs.

The size of the trees and their proximity to water made them easy marks for early loggers. The loop trail passes by several old stumps ringed with deep notches. These gouges in the bases of the trees were used to support springboards on which loggers stood in order to cut through the massive trunks.

Following the loop in a clockwise direction brings you within

Deer fern unfurling in spring

sight of an old homestead, and eventually you reach the shore of Lake Crescent. A wide clearing on the shore provides an exceptional view of the sparkling lake as well as to the jagged summit of Pyramid Peak. Also along the shore is a lone ponderosa pine that—not being native to this area—must have been planted by the homesteaders. Continuing along the loop, you head back into the forest, leaving the lake behind. As the lake view disappears, you encounter a long, tree-lined log just off the trail. This is one of the finest examples of a nurse log you'll find.

This newly created trail was begun by a work party staffed by the Washington Trails Association and the Klahhanes Hiking Club of Port Angeles. By 1996 up to 19 interpretive stations, as well as an information kiosk, will be installed by the Rob Reed and Lena Sharpe Memorial Foundation. The foundation was created in memory of two KCTS television reporters who died in a plane crash.

From Port Angeles, follow US Highway 101 west to Lake Crescent. Take the exit to the Storm King Ranger Station, about 3 miles beyond the east end of the lake. Turn right and drive toward the lake. Park in the ranger station parking lot. The trail leaves from the west end of the parking lot and after 0.3 mile reaches the main loop.

6
MARYMERE FALLS

Accessibility:	Moderate
Distance:	0.8 mile one way (only first 0.5 mile is accessible)
Gradient:	To 8%
Surface:	Dirt and gravel
When to go:	All year
Parking:	Designated
Restrooms:	Yes
Information:	Olympic National Park, (360) 452-4501

Wandering through lowland forest groves of ancient red cedar and Douglas fir, this trail follows a cool mountain stream to a nice river overlook. It is a peaceful place to visit, with plenty of wide turnouts

Marymere Falls trail

where you can pause and rest—or reflect on the beauty of the forest. Unfortunately, the barrier-free section ends at the overlook, well short of the river's edge and the pounding 90-foot waterfall.

From Port Angeles, drive west on US Highway 101 along the south shore of Lake Crescent. Turn right at the Lake Crescent Lodge sign and follow the road signs to the Storm King Visitor Center. The trailhead is located northeast of the parking area.

Leaving the trailhead, the trail drops down a short, narrow section before leveling off to pass through a tunnel under the highway. From there it meanders through the forest to the overlook. The steep descents at the beginning and toward the end of the route may be difficult for some users, so assistance may be required.

7

MADISON FALLS TRAIL

Accessibility: Easy
Distance: 200 yards
Gradient: Generally flat, some gentle slopes
Surface: Pavement
When to go: All year
Parking: Designated
Restrooms: Yes
Information: Olympic National Park, (360) 452-4501

Winding through a lush forest meadow and skirting a deep, ancient forest, this trail culminates at a stunning 100-foot waterfall.

Leaving the trailhead, you can enjoy the open meadow before reaching Madison Creek and paralleling it upstream. Should you decide to picnic here, you can use the small picnic table in the grassy meadow, just off the trail.

Midway up the trail is a bench that provides a good opportunity to rest and let the thunder of the nearby waterfall build your anticipation. The trail leads through a deep cleft in the mountainside and rounds one last bend; then, as the mist brushes your face, you see the splendid falls in all their thunderous glory. The large observation

Madison Falls

platform is the perfect spot to take in the breathtaking scene.

From Port Angeles, drive 7 miles west on US Highway 101 to the Elwha Valley sign. Turn left and continue 2 miles to the trailhead and parking area on the left.

8
HURRICANE HILL

Accessibility: Difficult
Distance: 0.5 mile round trip
Gradient: From 2% to 6%, parts 10% to 12%
Surface: Pavement and gravel
When to go: May–October
Parking: Designated
Restrooms: No
Information: Olympic National Park, (360) 452-4501

This trail entices you around corners and over hills with its magnificent views and alpine meadows. As for wildlife, keep an eye out

Hurricane Hill

for rabbits, marmots, deer, and the ever-present whiskey jacks—or camp-robber jays.

Follow US Highway 101 to midtown Port Angeles and turn south on Mount Angeles Road, following the signs to Hurricane Ridge, which is 17 miles south of the city limits. The trail begins from the parking area of the Hurricane Ridge Visitor Center.

This 7-foot-wide trail generally maintains grades of 2 to 6 percent, although in some places the grades briefly tilt to 10 percent. Care is essential on this trail because you will encounter some steep drop-offs with no guardrails. The entire trail is 1.5 miles long, but only the first 0.5 mile is accessible.

9
HURRICANE RIDGE MEADOW

Accessibility: Difficult
Distance: 0.5 mile network
Gradient: 25 feet at start/end to 15%, surface trails to 4%
Surface: Pavement
When to go: May–October
Parking: Designated
Restrooms: Yes (in the visitor center)
Information: Olympic National Park, (360) 452-4501

The opportunity to experience the alpine meadows on the ridge top—with the stunning vistas in the distance and the fragrant wildflowers underfoot—is worth the effort to get there. Even the short sections of 12 to 15 percent grade on the network of 7-foot wide paved trails should be visited. If that pitch sounds intimidating, remember that once up those initial grades leaving the parking area, you can explore a 0.5-mile network of fairly flat paved trails.

That's right: not just one but an entire network of trails meander through the wonders on the ridge. These trails earn top marks when it comes to scenery. On clear days you are rewarded with outstanding views of the Olympic Mountains—anchored by glacier-laden

Deer near Hurricane Ridge Lodge

Mount Olympus—to the south and the Strait of Juan de Fuca to the north. On truly clear days, the mountains of Vancouver Island are seen as shadows on the northern horizon.

Don't fret if the weather isn't so hospitable, as that will just force you to admire the views closer at hand, which may very likely include a few petite black-tailed deer and whistling marmots, which frequent this area. Be sure to visit the Hurricane Ridge Visitor Center, which offers accessible restrooms, exhibits on the upper level, and an auditorium where you can watch park orientation slide shows (large-text script is available for the program).

Follow US Highway 101 to midtown Port Angeles and turn south on Mount Angeles Road, following the signs to Hurricane Ridge, which is 17 miles south of the city limits. The trail begins from the parking area of the Hurricane Ridge Visitor Center.

10
PORT ANGELES
WATERFRONT TRAIL

Accessibility: Easy
Distance: 10 miles round trip
Gradient: Flat
Surface: First part pavement, last part dirt
When to go: All year
Parking: Designated
Restrooms: Yes
Information: Port Angeles Parks and Recreation, (360) 457-0411

Despite the dominance of the pulp mill, this trail along the water is charming. With views of Vancouver Island, Victoria, Ediz Hook, Mount Baker, and (on good days) Whitehorse and Three Fingers mountains, it is a restful but exhilarating trip. The basin is full of waterfowl and occasionally harbor seals and sea lions.

Follow US Highway 101 to downtown Port Angeles. Turn north on Lincoln Street (it's the street at the west end of the Red Lion Inn) and head toward the water. At the intersection of Lincoln Street and Railroad Street, you will find the parking area for the trail and the marine center.

Lights are being installed along the route, so don't rule out an evening visit. In the future, the trail will extend through the pulp mill property and further along the waterfront. The trail is paved most of the way. When the paved section ends, the dirt tread is excellent, and many users can easily negotiate it all the way to the mill's fence. There is a viewing platform near the end of the pavement, but it is not accessible.

Cormorant sculpture on the Port Angeles waterfront trail

From the starting point, the trail also goes west about 0.9 mile, basically as a sidewalk. The view on the west part of the trail is industrial space and log yards, definitely not the most exciting. Beyond this point, however, the trail widens into a 6- to 8-foot-wide paved trail. As you pass the marina, the views open into the inner harbor. The City of Port Angeles intends to extend this part of the trail through the Daishowa mill and onto Ediz Hook. Some of this construction should take place prior to this book's publication. The views will be comparable to the east section of the trail when looking into the Strait of Juan de Fuca. However, the view of the Olympic Mountains to the south will be different and striking.

This trail will eventually be about 10 miles in length. It will run from the end of Ediz Hook to Morse Creek, on the east side of the Rayonier mill, at the start of Ediz Hook. Currently the trail extends from the Daishowa mill to the Rayonier mill. From the starting point described in the directions, the trail runs on an old railroad grade to the Rayonier pulp mill to the east.

11

DUNGENESS NATIONAL WILDLIFE REFUGE

Accessibility:	Moderate
Distance:	0.75 mile round trip
Gradient:	To 2%
Surface:	Gravel and dirt (pavement planned)
When to go:	All year
Parking:	Designated
Restrooms:	Yes
Information:	Dungeness National Wildlife Refuge, (360) 753-9467

This trail ends at a viewing pad overlooking an immense natural spit running 5 miles out into the Strait of Juan de Fuca. Actually, there are two spits—a smaller one to the east reaches almost all the way out to the main Dungeness Spit, creating a relatively calm,

Dungeness Spit

protected bay that is home to thousands of migratory waterfowl, shorebirds, and aquatic animals.

From Sequim, drive west for 6 miles on US Highway 101 and turn right on Kitchen-Dick Lane. In 3 miles turn right on Lotzgesell Road and left again at the sign for the recreational area and refuge.

The trail on the spit itself isn't accessible, but the route to the overlook is moderately so (the dirt and gravel surface creates some rough terrain). The paving of the route, scheduled for completion in the mid- to late 1990s, will make it easily accessible for all.

The refuge has done a great job with the parking area and the restrooms; even the outdoor water fountain accommodates wheel-chair users! Make sure you bring your binoculars, and use them at the overlook to get a close look at the visiting great blue herons and bald eagles that are fond of roosting in the trees just across the forested gulch. When you've had your fill of them, turn the binocs seaward and look along the western edge of the spit for sea lions and even the occasional whale.

On the return up the hill to the parking area, you can justify frequent rest stops as you look for the songbirds and Stellar's jays that populate the forest here.

12
RAILROAD BRIDGE

Accessibility:	Easy
Distance:	1 mile round trip
Gradient:	To 3%
Surface:	Pavement and boardwalk
When to go:	All year
Parking:	Usable
Restrooms:	No
Information:	Clallam County Parks Department, (360) 452-7831

Close to Sequim, this park offers a quiet, wild setting. A highlight of the trail is the stunning scenery, which includes views of an old-fashioned wooden railroad bridge, the Dungeness River, its shoreline, and a horse trail. Traversing pastures and woods to the wetland environment on the banks of the Dungeness River, the birdwatcher in you should get a lot of enjoyment from this trail. In addition to the multitude of songbirds and jays, you may see redtailed hawks soaring in the sky. If it's a clear day, take a good look at the tops of the trees: the hawks like to perch on high lookouts almost as much as they like to soar on the thermal winds.

Old wooden trestle over the Dungeness River (Photo: Greg Ball)

From Sequim, drive 1.6 miles west on US Highway 101. Turn right onto Mill Road, at Flipper's Restaurant, and continue 0.6 mile before turning right onto East Runnion Road. Drive 0.4 mile to the intersection of East Runnion Road and Heath Road. On your immediate right is a small paved driveway with a tiny wood sign for the trail. Turn down the driveway; the parking area is to the left.

The trail is wide and in great condition, with turnouts and benches on a gradual ramp that extends over the wooded wetlands to the railroad bridge. Anglers enjoy casting for trout from the turnouts, although the railing height is not convenient for wheelchair users.

This is a nice spot for viewing fall colors or for catching the roar of a river during spring thaw.

13
SEAL ROCK

Accessibility: Difficult
Distance: 0.25 mile loop
Gradient: From 5% to 9%
Surface: Pavement
When to go: All year
Parking: Designated
Restrooms: Yes
Information: USFS Quilcene Ranger District, (360) 765-3368

Shellfish fanatics, take note: the Seal Rock Campground, tucked away along the western shore of Hood Canal, happens to be one of the few national forest campgrounds located on salt water and blessed with harvestable oysters.

From Quilcene, drive 8.5 miles south on US Highway 101. Watch for the Seal Rock Campground turnoff—the trailhead is located inside the campground.

Though it stays off the beach, this paved trail takes advantage of the marine environment, offering an accessible viewing platform that reaches over the beach and plenty of interpretive signage along the way to explain the flora and fauna. The natural sea life isn't the only impressive scenery, though; this is also a wonderful place to watch the massive metal fish of Bangor. Trident nuclear submarines are frequently seen breaching here as they head into port.

This trail earns difficult access marks from us because it climbs to a 9 percent grade. The trail is paved and varies from 4 to 6 feet in width. If you plan to harvest oysters, be sure to check the regulations—seasonal closures are common at short notice due to changing tidal conditions, which can cause high levels of a natural toxin to be present in the oysters. These closures are generally brief, though, and when they are not in effect, the Hood Canal oysters offer a fine barbecue dinner in camp.

14
ISLAND LAKE

Accessibility:	Easy
Distance:	1 mile round trip
Gradient:	Flat
Surface:	Pavement
When to go:	All year
Parking:	Designated
Restrooms:	Yes
Information:	Kitsap County Parks, (360) 895-3895

This paved trail runs within the park, linking the beach through woods to the community meeting hall. It offers good views of the water. The lake is surrounded by new urban development, and the park is an urban county park, but it offers a nice lakeside trail graced with flocks of waterfowl and large stands of second-growth timber. The park is well maintained and enjoyed by a diverse group of trail users, including roller-bladers, joggers, walkers, and bicyclists. Accessible parking and restrooms are located at both the community center and beach area (about 0.5 mile apart). Beyond the swimming area, the trail crosses the inlet stream and forks: the right fork goes more steeply uphill to a group picnic pavilion, while the left fork eventually winds back to the swimming area. This is a nice trail on which to test your skills and endurance before you go on to more difficult trails. The surrounding area is developing rapidly.

From Bremerton, take State Route 304 to State Route 3. Go north to the Newberry Hill Road exit. Take the exit east to Silverdale Way, continue north on Silverdale Way for approximately 3 miles (this takes you through the town of Silverdale), and eventually turn right onto Bennington Drive. Follow Bennington Drive for almost 0.5 mile. The entrance to Island Lake Park is on the right side of the road. Park in front of the community meeting hall. An alternative that avoids the sprawl of Silverdale is to take State Route 303 or Warren Avenue out of Bremerton. Just after milepost 8 on State Route 303, take the Silverdale Way exit. Turn right at the end of the exit ramp onto Silverdale Way and proceed about 2 miles to Bennington Drive. Turn right on Bennington Drive, and proceed almost 0.5 mile to the park on the right.

15
HOOD CANAL WETLANDS

Accessibility:	Easy
Distance:	3.8 miles round trip
Gradient:	To 3%
Surface:	Gravel and boardwalk
When to go:	All year
Parking:	Designated
Restrooms:	Yes (in the community center and halfway down main loop trail)
Information:	Theler Memorial Community Center, (360) 275-4898

Located at the base of Hood Canal, this network of trails is an all-season hit, but be prepared for the weather! You'll meet fresh breezes (or turbulent gusts!) on the open boardwalks and dike trails. If the winds are bearable, though, don't miss the opportunity to get out and enjoy the exceptional vistas from the high boardwalk piers and dikes. Lush greenery surrounds the route, but the brush is kept carefully clipped to provide open, unobstructed views.

From Belfair, drive west on State Route 3 and watch for signs to the wetlands and Theler Community Center, located on the north side of the road. Park at Theler Community Center. The trailhead and information kiosk are to the left of the main building.

Leaving the community center on a gentle downhill slope, the trail crosses a bridge and leads into a freshwater wetland environment. To get a good look at where you are, cross the open meadow (saving the trails to your right for later exploration) and head toward the saltwater. Notice how the landscape makes a dramatic change from a freshwater wetland to an intertidal saltwater estuary. The boardwalk pier takes you straight out, over the prairie of bunchgrass, sedge, and rushes lined with muddy waterways. Piled amid the vegetation are stacks of driftwood, left high and dry by the ferocious winter storms that pound against the shore. At the end of the pier is a roomy viewing area. Remember to bring binoculars if you want a good look at the array of birds and animals that live in the estuary.

Returning the way you came, take the first trail on your left and wander at leisure along the dike trails, which were originally built by a local kennel club for training hunting dogs. The freshwater ponds, constructed by the club, remain popular with ducks and other birds. If you are quiet and careful, you can spot many of the birds, frogs, and other small creatures that live here.

The trail also passes farmland, while in the distance here you can see a trailer park and the highway. The sharp contrasts offer a good view of how land use changes over time and how human beings dramatically shape and reshape their surroundings. Interpretive signs offer further details about this particular ecosystem and the human impact on it.

When you reach the Union River, look for otter "slides," as well as signs of beavers, muskrats, raccoons, and coyotes. Here you can see birds aplenty, as they feast on the rich offerings of the river. Following the river, you may be relieved to spot the accessible restroom.

Just past the restroom and the adjacent gravel viewing area is a spur trail to the left that is worth some exploration. There is a view spot where you can contemplate a quiet turn in the river, and just around the corner is a quiet, marshy meadow surrounded by second-growth woodland. Upon your return to the freshwater ponds, turn left along the trail on which you began. Here a small boardwalk slips through the last surprise, a swamp with western red cedar and red alder. Look for a nesting box and pileated woodpeckers on this part of the trail.

16
PETE'S CREEK

Accessibility:	Difficult
Distance:	0.5 mile
Gradient:	One steep (10%) pitch, then flat
Surface:	Compacted gravel, dirt
When to go:	April–October
Parking:	Designated
Restrooms:	Yes
Information:	USFS Quinault Ranger District, (360) 288-2525

This trail starts in a wonderful old-growth forest and emerges into a former clear-cut that is now graced with young, five- to ten-year-old Douglas firs. The accessible part of the trail ends on a bluff. The trail continues steeply down to the Humptulips River but is no longer accessible. From the young forest, enjoy views back into the Colonel Bob Wilderness and the upper reaches of Pete's Creek. An interesting feature of this area is that you can see old-growth and second-growth forests side by side and compare the two ecosystems.

From Hoquiam, drive 27 miles north on US Highway 101 to a junction with Donkey Creek Road (Forest Service Road 22). Turn right and continue 8.2 miles east on Donkey Creek Road before turning left onto Forest Service Road 2204. Follow Road 2204 10.9 miles to the trailhead on the left. Call before you go; this trail is often wet and muddy, making it difficult to travel.

17
MIMA MOUNDS

Accessibility: Easy
Distance: 0.5 mile loop
Gradient: Flat
Surface: Pavement
When to go: All year
Parking: Usable
Restrooms: Yes
Information: DNR Chehalis, (360) 753-3410

As you drive to the parking area, you catch your first sight of the mounds, hidden in the forest. Starting down the trail, you emerge into a prairie that looks like a giant's sandbox. The prairie floor is literally covered with circular mounds 4 to 5 feet in height. For

Along the trail to the Mima Mounds

Mima Mounds

those seeking an early-season trip, spring wildflowers here are out-standing.

From Olympia, drive south on Interstate 5 to exit 95. Take this exit and drive 3 miles west to Littlerock. From the stop sign at the outskirts of town, go straight through the small business district and follow the sign to Capital Forest on 128th Street. Drive to the stop sign 0.7 mile after leaving Littlerock and turn right where a sign points toward Mima Mounds. Turn left after 0.8 mile and en-ter the Mima Mounds area. Follow the signs to the trailhead.

Scattered around the trail are eleven interpretive stations; one sign explains two popular theories about the mounds that have survived scientific scrutiny. One is a geological theory; the other has to do with hypothetical, now extinct, giant gophers that may have burrowed here. The mounds were first sighted by Captain

Charles Wilkes in 1840. Since his visit, no scientific explanation has been agreed upon.

Trail signs direct traffic in a counterclockwise direction. At about the halfway point, there is a side trail with a ramp leading to an observation platform. Take this route for a better view of the enigmatic panorama. There are benches at the start of the trail and at the observation deck. After the ramp spur, the main trail continues. Here you wander through a young forest growing on some of the mounds as it encroaches on the prairie.

There are two points where tree roots have caused the pavement to buckle. These buckles may be a problem for wheelchair users.

18
LONG BEACH BOARDWALK

Accessibility:	Easy
Distance:	0.8 mile round trip
Gradient:	Flat
Surface:	Boardwalk
When to go:	All year
Parking:	Designated (north end)
Restrooms:	Yes (south end)
Information:	City of Long Beach Parks Department, (360) 642-4421

Forget the Atlantic City boardwalk with tourist shops and other casinos. This is what every beachfront boardwalk should strive to be.

Here in Long Beach is the opportunity to enjoy an unobstructed view of the Pacific breakers over native grass–covered sand dunes. Even the limited glitz of Washington's beach towns is almost hidden from view as you travel along this wide boardwalk. The view to the west is entirely sand and ocean. To the east you can see a wide expanse of beach grass and stunted conifers. On the far horizon are the timbered hills of the coast mountains. The boardwalk has several interpretive stations with benches and signs explaining the area's habitat, beach life, history, and shipwrecks. The boardwalk is lit at night, making for impressive and romantic summer evenings.

Long Beach boardwalk during the annual kite festival (Photo: Marge and Ted Mueller)

From Montesano, drive south on State Route 107 to US Highway 101. Continue south on Highway 101 to the intersection with State Route 103 (Pacific Highway) in Seaview, and head north on Route 103 to the first stoplight, at Bolstad Road. Turn left onto Bolstad Road and continue about 3 blocks to the parking area.

The road leading to the boardwalk is hard sand and could be a problem for wheelchair users—especially those with narrow tires. On the north end, a paved sidewalk leads to the boardwalk. Adjoining this sidewalk is another paved strip with five reserved, accessible parking spaces. The drifting sand often covers the accessible designation markers. Look closely! The restrooms at the south end are accessible, but to reach them you must cross the hard sand road and about 50 feet of loose sand and gravel. After your visit, consider telling the land manager that this short sidewalk needs to be paved in order for the restrooms to be truly accessible.

19

M ⚘ ☀ 🍂 ❄

JULIA BUTLER HANSEN
NATIONAL WILDLIFE REFUGE

Accessibility: Moderate
Distance: 4 miles loop trip
Gradient: Generally flat, to 8.5% at entrance/exit
Surface: Gravel
When to go: All year
Parking: Usable
Restrooms: No (restrooms planned)
Information: Refuge Manager, (360) 795-3915

As the name implies, this trail leads to countless opportunities to witness many forms of wildlife in their natural habitat. From September through November, dawn to dusk is the best time for viewing deer and elk, while from October through March, geese and ducks are found gathered together in huge flotillas, idling away the cold winter months. But that's not all. Sandhill cranes stop here briefly during their spring and fall migrations, and coyotes, beavers, hawks, and countless other small species make this their permanent home.

The trail traverses old farm fields over a gravel road, then turns left along the Columbia River for 0.75 mile before turning at the mouth of the Elochman River back to the parking area. The views of the Columbia and Elochman rivers are a big attraction.

From Longview, follow State Route 4 west to Cathlamet and 2 miles beyond to Steamboat Slough Road, the entrance to the refuge. Watch for the bridge over the Elochman River. The entrance is on your left, just west of the bridge.

Ignore the sign directing hikers to the right-hand side of the parking area, and turn left for the gentlest grade to the trailhead. Also beware the tight wigwag gate at the trail entrance. This is narrow and was somewhat overgrown with grass at the time of our visit. You may wish to call the refuge a few days prior to your trip, as the office is not always staffed. Refuge staff are willing to assist people over the grade from the parking area, and can unlock the main gate if the wigwag gate is not negotiable.

The refuge was created in 1972 from farms once owned by twenty different families. It is home to the last herd of Columbia white-tailed deer, a subspecies once thought extinct. It is one of two subspecies of the white-tailed deer currently endangered in the United States. Cows are used as a maintenance tool on the refuge during half the year, since grass in this region grows more than 6 feet yearly, but they are kept off the trail by fences, so they pose no problem to visitors.

The presence of the cows, in fact, emphasizes the fact that this is not a wilderness—it is more like an old farm gone to seed or a domesticated area slowly converting back to wilderness. Alongside the domestic cattle, wild deer and elk feed. Wild geese and ducks fly overhead, and wild predators hunt for their livelihood.

The refuge is situated in a valley bottom, and the low rolling hills nearby catch the clouds moving inland off the Pacific Ocean. Dusk brings muskrats and fish out in the slough, and hawks overhead. The autumn is exciting when the elk visit these wide meadows and the big bulls bugle their love songs to their mates and their threats to potential rivals.

Don't forget, though, that the refuge is an all-season delight. The trail should be accessible in all but the rainiest weather, when puddles may pose problems. No matter when you go, you will find plenty to see and experience.

NORTH CASCADES

20
DECEPTION PASS
SAND DUNE TRAIL

E 🌷 ☀️ 🍂 ❄️

Accessibility: Easy
Distance: 0.8 mile round trip
Gradient: Flat
Surface: Pavement
When to go: All year
Parking: Usable
Restrooms: Yes
Information: Washington State Parks and Recreation, (360) 902-8563

This trail has it all: views of Cranberry Lake and nearby wetlands to the east, the Olympic Mountains to the southwest, and the San Juan Islands to the northwest, as well as interpretive signs explaining the dune environment. In the winter you're likely to spot many bald eagles and other birds.

The park is found on the extreme north end of Whidbey Island. From Anacortes, drive south on State Route 20. Just south of the Deception Pass Bridge, turn west into the park entrance. From there follow the main road 0.1 mile to a stop sign. Turn right and continue 0.8 mile, passing through one intersection, to the entrance to a large parking area. Traffic goes one way through the parking lot (right), and at the far south end of the parking lot is the trailhead.

Since there are no designated disabled parking spaces and this is a popular park, parking may be difficult. What parking is available is ill-defined and surfaced with sand and loose cobbles, so it may be necessary for wheelchair users to unload at the trailhead or to have assistance from the parking area. Also, there is a sign imbedded directly in the middle of the entrance to the trail. This may be a slight problem for people with wider-than-average wheelchairs. Beyond the entrance, however, there are no more obstacles.

The trail proceeds to a building with accessible restrooms (which are closed in the winter). Beyond this point the trail separates and makes a loop. Going in a clockwise direction, you enter a beach

Fog-covered Artist Point and Mount Shuksan (Trail no. 24)

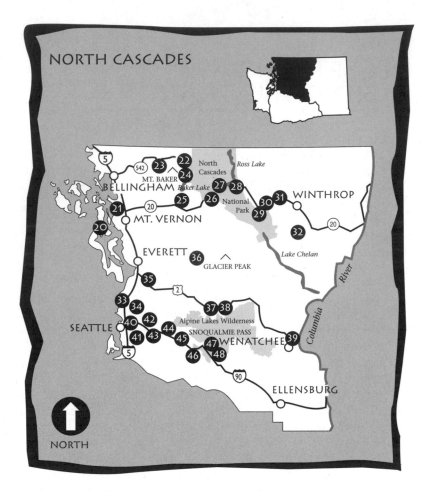

NORTH CASCADES

542 MT. BAKER
BELLINGHAM   Baker Lake
North Cascades
Ross Lake
WINTHROP
MT. VERNON
National Park
20
EVERETT
GLACIER PEAK
Lake Chelan
Columbia River
2
Alpine Lakes Wilderness
SEATTLE
SNOQUALMIE PASS
WENATCHEE
5
90
ELLENSBURG

NORTH

forest with Douglas firs and occasional spruce. The predominant view is eastward over Cranberry Lake and a wetland area. There are nonaccessible turnouts to picnic areas.

Near the south end is a larger turnout on compact dirt and gravel. The angle to the viewing platform a short distance farther is slightly steeper. There is, unfortunately, a 3-inch vertical difference between the higher platform and the trail surface, so assistance may be required. The platform, which looks out over a vast wetland, should be excellent for bird watching in the spring.

Returning to the main trail, the path turns toward the ocean beach and forks at another viewing point. The left fork leads to the viewing platform. Again the branch trail is not paved and is a little steeper. It leads to a level (though short) boardwalk with splendid views of the beach and crashing waves. You can see the San Juans and Olympics from here.

Both of these turnouts are worth the extra effort to access them. The trail continues, meandering through dunes until it returns to the restroom area. When we visited, a magnificent lone eagle watched us intently from its perch in a nearby fir.

Sand dune trail, Deception Pass State Park

21
PADILLA BAY

Accessibility: Easy to moderate
Distance: 5.75 miles round trip (total of all trails)
Gradient: Generally flat, one hill on one trail up to 8%
Surface: Gravel
When to go: All year; Wednesday–Sunday, 10:00 A.M.–5:00 P.M.
Parking: Designated
Restrooms: Yes
Information: Padilla Bay National Estuarine Research Reserve Manager, (360) 428-1558

The Padilla Bay Reserve and the Breazeale Interpretive Center are a real treat, even in blustery or rainy weather. The interpretive center has an accessible viewing deck. Inside the center, which is entirely accessible, you are treated to enthusiastic staff and many displays about the area's ecosystem and natural history. These include salt-water aquariums that provide "windows" to the bay's abundant underwater life. There is also a "Hands On" room for sensory exploration. If you are so inclined, call in advance for information on their many presentations and classes. Before you leave, inquire about trail maps, interpretive guides, and the possibilities of checking out identification guides and/or binoculars. Important: You need to check out a key for disabled access to the Shore Trail!

From Mount Vernon, follow Interstate 5 north to exit 230. Take this exit and follow State Route 20 west for 5.2 miles before turning right on Bow Edison Road, which becomes Farm to Market Road. At 8.1 miles from I-5, turn left on Josh Wilson Road. At 9.7 miles, you reach a three-way intersection. Turn right on Bayview-Edison Road, and at 10.5 miles the center is on the right.

The 0.8-mile Upland Trail is paved and easy to access for about half its length. After meandering from the parking area, you find yourself in meadows and woodlands. If you stay to the right at the trail's fork you reach a sheltered view spot. From here the trail is inaccessible. The left fork of the trail ranges from difficult to inaccessible. It is gravel, in many places grown over by grass, and fea-

Padilla Bay trail

tures steep hills. The ridge top is covered in mixed forest, broken by a few pastures and meadows. As the trail loops down toward the interpretive center, you enjoy good views of the bay. Here, though, you are again faced with an inaccessible section of trail. The long, but pleasant, option is to retrace your path.

The 0.28-mile paved trail to the view deck is easy to access and well engineered. Here, again, you travel through meadow before slipping under the road to a beautiful view deck. The beach is inaccessible from here, but this spot offers an excellent opportunity for viewing migratory and native waterfowl.

To reach the 2.25-mile Shore Trail, which is Padilla Bay's main trail attraction, drive 3.3 miles south on Bayview-Edison Road. The southernmost parking area has a reserved parking spot and offers direct access to the trail, which is an excellent dike-top path. With unobstructed views of a tidal marsh, two sloughs, and open mud flats, you are likely to see a wide variety of waterfowl, raptors, and other birds.

While the gravel lifted our accessibility rating to moderate, the trail's compact surface is unlikely to present problems for anyone. Picnic tables, benches, and turnouts invite you to pause and take in the surroundings.

22
PICTURE LAKE

Accessibility:	Easy
Distance:	0.25 mile loop
Gradient:	To 2%
Surface:	Pavement
When to go:	July–October
Parking:	Designated
Restrooms:	No
Information:	USFS Mount Baker Ranger District, (360) 856-5700

Picture Lake is said to be among the most picturesque nature spots in the country! Reflecting all of Mount Shuksan's glory on cloudless days, the alpine lake is a crystal-blue gem cradled in the wildflower-filled Heather Meadows Area.

From Bellingham, follow Interstate 5 north to exit 255. Take this exit and continue east on State Route 542 through Maple Falls and Glacier to Heather Meadows, found at the start of a one-way loop road just before you reach the upper ski area.

Nestled in the Mount Baker Recreation Area, the trail accessing this stunning landscape is a flat, smooth path that circles the lake with various piers and a few narrower side paths. In the early autumn, you can gather blueberries and huckleberries along the route. This 0.25-mile trail is ideal for everyone. It holds no surprises, only beauty.

Mount Shuksan reflected in Picture Lake

23
AUSTIN PASS PICNIC AREA /FIRE AND ICE I AND II

E/D ☀️ 🌿

Accessibility: First 0.13 mile easy, last 0.13 mile difficult
Distance: First part 0.25 mile loop, last part 0.13 mile round trip
Gradient: First part 3%, last part to 25%
Surface: Pavement and gravel
When to go: July–October
Parking: Designated
Restrooms: Yes
Information: USFS Mount Baker Ranger District, (360) 856-5700

The best part of hiking a trail through alpine meadows in the Cascades is that, with good timing, you can feast on nature's finest candy—mountain blueberries!

This trail offers that opportunity as it passes through beautiful, wide alpine meadows. The blueberries are ripe in September, but don't despair if you get here early—a multitude of wildflowers bloom throughout the summer, painting the meadows with their glorious colors. The scenery is further enhanced by the looming walls of columnar andesite, a distinctive rock formation left in the wake of volcanic activity thousands of years ago. As you near the formations, interpretive signs explain the geological features. With the exception of the interpretive boards, this trail is not signed, so it may be difficult to find.

From Bellingham, follow Interstate 5 north to exit 255. Take this exit and continue east on State Route 542 through Maple Falls, past the Mount Baker ski area, to the Austin Pass Picnic Area.

From the parking area, follow the signs to the Austin Pass Visitor Center, where the trail begins. The first portion maintains a 3 percent grade as it meanders about 0.13 mile into the Bagley Lake area. At the end of the asphalt, just before the lookout point, the trail cuts down and left into a meadow.

From here the trail must be rated difficult to access. The first

Bagley Lake and Table Mountain

15 feet of the trail are very rigorous, with a 24 percent grade, and the trail narrows to barely 3 feet across. There are several obstacles that require some maneuvering, but soon enough you come upon a small fishing pier, the perfect spot for admiring beautiful Bagley Lake. The trail continues beyond the lake, but this area is inaccessible, as the grade increases dramatically.

24
ARTIST RIDGE
AND ARTIST POINT

Accessibility: Easy
Distance: Both trails 0.25 mile round trip
Gradient: To 5%
Surface: Pavement
When to go: August–October
Parking: Designated
Restrooms: Yes
Information: USFS Mount Baker Ranger District, (360) 856-5700

Knowing that artists seek the most beautiful areas to reproduce in their work, the name of this trail suggests it might be a stun-

Mount Baker from Artist Point

ning place to visit. That suggestion is absolutely correct.

Artist Ridge is an indisputably beautiful spot located on an arm of Mount Shuksan in the Heather Meadows Area. This paved trail winds along the ridge to a lookout point, where you have a perfect vantage of not only Mount Baker but also her gorgeous neighbor, Mount Shuksan, and the deep valley of Swift Creek. This is a good place to stop and snack on the local wild berries—mountain blueberries, huckleberries, and the occasional wild strawberry—while luxuriating in the warm afternoon sun.

From Bellingham, follow Interstate 5 north to exit 255. Take this exit and continue east on State Route 542 through Maple Falls and Glacier to the end of the road, which is Artist Point.

The trail begins at the parking area and branches immediately at the place where the Artist Point trail begins to wind around to its lookout point on the mountains. The Artist Point trail's gradient is 5 percent, while the Artist Ridge trail has a minimal grade of 1 percent. Both trails are very accessible.

25
SHADOW OF THE SENTINELS

Accessibility: Easy
Distance: 0.5 mile loop
Gradient: Generally flat, to 8%
Surface: Boardwalk and pavement
When to go: All year
Parking: Designated
Restrooms: Yes
Information: USFS Mount Baker Ranger District, (360) 856-5700

The Sentinels are trees that sprouted well before Christopher Columbus set sail across the Atlantic. For half a millennium these trees have grown in the shadow of Mount Baker, and this trail offers a chance to experience their grandeur. The one-way loop slopes gently through the magnificent 500-year-old forest, a reminder of what the area must have looked like prior to the extensive logging you must drive through to get here.

From Mount Vernon, follow Interstate 5 north to exit 230. Take this exit and drive east on State Route 20 to the Baker Lake Road junction. Turn north on Baker Lake Road and continue 2.5 miles

The Sentinels

beyond the turnoff to Mount Baker National Recreation Area. The trailhead is on the right.

The well-engineered trail alternates sections of asphalt with boardwalks over the undulating terrain. Remember, the boardwalks get slippery in the rain. As you hike along the route, watch for nurse logs among the moss-draped trees. These are old, fallen trees that act as "nursemaids" by providing a source of nutrients and footing for newly sprouted trees. As the new trees grow, their roots encircle and embrace the old, decomposing tree, using its store of nutrients and minerals to fuel their own growth. In this way, the ancient forest continues to thrive and grow. The fourteen interpretive signs along the trail explain the dynamics of old-growth forests.

As wonderful as the trail experience is, a large part of this trail's lure is the drive after leaving State Route 20—despite the numerous unsightly clear-cuts. With clear weather, you have stunning views of craggy, snow-capped peaks, as well as glacier-covered Mount Baker and Mount Shuksan.

26
STERLING MUNRO

Accessibility:	Easy
Distance:	110 yards
Gradient:	Generally flat, some gentle slopes
Surface:	Boardwalk
When to go:	All year
Parking:	Designated
Restrooms:	Yes
Information:	North Cascades National Park, (360) 856-5700

Don't let the length of this trail deceive you into thinking it's not worth a stop. It is a splendid little trail that winds through a shaded forest and ends at a large viewing deck, offering stunning views of the Picket Range.

From Newhalem, follow State Route 20 to the North Cascades

Visitor Center. The trailhead is behind and to the left of the center.

The trail's namesake served as chief of staff to Senator Henry Jackson for a number of years. Munro loved the wilderness and worked hard to preserve and protect it. The trail was named after him because the Picket Range was one of his favorite views.

The visitor center itself makes a worthwhile stop. It offers exhibits, maps, a slide presentation, weather information, a small bookstore, and informational brochures on the North Cascades area.

27
TRAIL OF THE CEDARS

Accessibility:	Difficult
Distance:	0.5 mile loop
Gradient:	Flat, short grades to 13%
Surface:	Gravel
When to go:	All year
Parking:	Usable
Restrooms:	No
Information:	Seattle City Light, (206) 684-3884

Passing through a grove of ancient cedars, this trail offers a glimpse into another world. Trees of this type—towering cedars of unbelievable girth—were at the foundation of many native American societies. The tribes found they could make just about anything they needed from the strong, straight-grained wood or the fibrous bark—houses, baskets, fishing spears, beds, canoes.

From Mount Vernon, follow Interstate 5 north to exit 230. Take this exit and drive east on State Route 20 through Newhalem. Turn south at the old steam engine and general store sign. The trailhead is only 2 blocks from State Route 20.

The trail begins at a point directly across the street from a paved parking area. The trail leads across a suspension bridge that bears a plaque proclaiming, "My dad built this bridge." During their annual runs, it is possible to see spawning salmon at the bridge, but their passage further upriver is blocked by the series of dams.

After crossing the bridge, the trail continues along the river as it weaves through the grove of ancient red cedars. It has two short sections that climb and descend steeply, so wheelchair users may need assistance.

Suspension bridge, Trail of the Cedars (Photo: Dave Freeh, Seattle City Light)

28
HAPPY CREEK

Accessibility: Moderate
Distance: 0.3 mile round trip
Gradient: To 8%
Surface: Boardwalk
When to go: June–October, when SR 20 is open
Parking: Designated
Restrooms: Yes
Information: North Cascades National Park, (360) 856-5700

On the drive to the trailhead, enjoy spectacular views of the North Cascades, including the Picket Range, Hozomeen, Colonial Peak, Paul Bunyan's Stump, and Ross Lake.

From Mount Vernon, follow Interstate 5 north to exit 230. Take

Happy Creek trail

Elevated boardwalk along Happy Creek (Photo: USFS, Methow Valley Ranger District)

this exit and drive east through Newhalem for 14.5 miles to the trailhead.

The trail loops through a heavily wooded area, at one point following a beautiful little stream. While the trail is entirely board-walk, it ascends or descends virtually the entire way. The grade never reaches above 8 percent, but the continual up and down may make this trail more challenging than it appears. Also, the boardwalk is slippery in wet weather.

29
RAINY LAKE

E ☀ 🌿

Accessibility:	Easy
Distance:	1.8 miles round trip
Gradient:	Flat, to 8%
Surface:	Pavement
When to go:	June–October, when SR 20 is open
Parking:	Designated
Restrooms:	Yes
Information:	USFS Winthrop District, (509) 996-2266

This is what natural trails are all about: alpine meadows, towering glacier-covered peaks, gurgling creeks, sparkling lakes, and a route that is accessible to all. This is one of the very best barrier-free trails in Washington.

The trail begins on the south side of the summit of Rainy Pass. From Newhalem, drive east for 3.7 miles on State Route 20.

There is no parking at the trailhead, but you may unload there. A parking loop has three designated spots. An asphalt trail runs inside the loop to the trailhead.

Starting just off the highway, the trail runs along the Pacific Crest Trail for nearly a mile before turning to follow a tumbling creek to Rainy Lake. The trail pauses at an overlook of the lake and Lyall Glacier, high above.

The lake is a sparkling blue jewel set in a steep-walled box canyon—or cirque. The cirque was formed by the forward action of the glacier pushing against the rocky slope before the ice river began its present retreat. Notice that although there is no evidence of logging, the trees are relatively small, a result of the high elevation and difficult growing conditions. At the overlook you can sometimes see a seasonal waterfall crashing down the cirque wall. The trail has a log safety barrier on its downhill side, with interpretive signs and benches along the way.

Rainy Pass was the sixth mountain pass to be crossed by a highway in Washington state. The first rough road was blasted through in late 1968. State Route 20 was opened to the public five years later,

Rainy Lake reflecting the surrounding mountains (Photo: USFS, Methow Valley Ranger District)

providing access to perhaps the most beautiful mountain scenery in the Northwest. Where Rainy Lake was once accessible only by a long, rough pack trail, the lake now lies within 0.25 mile of the highway.

Don't miss this splendid trail and alpine scenery.

30
WASHINGTON PASS OVERLOOK

Accessibility:	Easy
Distance:	0.15 mile round trip
Gradient:	Flat
Surface:	Pavement
When to go:	June–October, or if SR 20 is open
Parking:	Designated
Restrooms:	Yes
Information:	USFS Winthrop District, (509) 996-2266

Don't discount this path just because it is short. The beauty and grandeur found along the route is unsurpassed by most trails ten times its length.

Start off with an easy path through broad fields of wildflowers and berry patches. Savor the juicy sweetness of mountain blueberries and wild strawberries as you luxuriate in the brilliant splashes of color furnished by the paintbrush, lupine, spreading phlox, penstemons, glacier lilies, and other flowers in the area.

After bathing your senses in the natural wonders close at hand, move down the trail for panoramic views of stunning peaks. You'll find the best views from a spectacular viewpoint at the trail's end. It overlooks Washington Pass and presents great views of Silver Star, the Wine Spires, Early Winter Spires, and Liberty Bell. These jagged granite peaks are the crown jewels of one of the most rugged, pristine alpine areas in the nation.

But the high-elevation summits of the North Cascades aren't the only scenery on the horizon. The much drier east side of the

Liberty Bell from the Washington Pass overlook (Photo: USFS, Methow Valley Ranger District)

Cascades begins to be apparent at this viewpoint. Most notable is the change in the forest below the viewpoint. The moist, old-growth cedar and hemlock of Western Washington blend with the dry pine and spruce of Eastern Washington here, presenting a unique, stunningly diverse forest.

With all this scenery and natural wonder, it is no wonder that visitors deem this vista an area unmatched by anything else in the state. So make sure you bring your camera.

From Winthrop, drive west on State Route 20 to Washington Pass. The trailhead is north of the highway at milepost 162.

31
LONE FIR

Accessibility:	Paved part easy, dirt part difficult
Distance:	Paved part 0.8 mile, entire trail 2 miles round trip
Gradient:	To 5%
Surface:	Pavement and dirt
When to go:	June–October
Parking:	Usable
Restrooms:	Yes (in campground)
Information:	USFS Winthrop District, (509) 996-2266

This woodsy, winding route includes four old-fashioned log bridges with great creek and wash views. Interpretive signs describe the surrounding ecosystem and the forces that affect this mix of streamside and forest settings. The paved portion of the trail leads you to wonderful views from a bridge over Early Winters Creek.

From Winthrop, drive west on State Route 20 for 23.5 miles. The trailhead is found in the Lone Fir Campground, on the left (south) side of the highway. It is well signed before and at the turnoff. The trailhead is on the right, just beyond the entrance on the one-way campground loop road. Note: The accessible restrooms are at the other end of the one-way loop road, just before you reach the entrance.

The many trees—fir, pine, and hemlock, as well as deciduous

varieties—make the route's name, Lone Fir, a mystery. The trail, which follows the route over Washington Pass commonly used by native Americans and nineteenth-century trappers, prospectors, and settlers, begins in the campground. Crossing a small creek bed and then Pine Creek on plank bridges, one can see flowering currant, ferns, and maple along the path. Look for blue larkspur blooms in season. Continue through an open grove of pine and fir trees ranging from 3 and 4 feet to an occasional 20 or 30 feet in height. The

Early Winters Creek (Photo: USFS, Methow Valley Ranger District)

forest floor is carpeted with kinnikinnick. The Needles, rising 7,400 feet above, are visible through the treetops to the right, while Vasilki Ridge makes appearances to your left.

At about 0.25 mile, the trail reaches a grove of larger trees and begins an uphill grade that may require assistance for wheelchair users. Continuing in shade, you can hear the sound of water to the left until, as the path descends, you see glimpses of Early Winters Creek.

At the lowest point of the grade, the trail reaches a plank bridge across Early Winters Creek. Spaced handrails afford a clear view of the water bubbling over its bed of golden-colored rocks. The accessible portion of the trail ends with the bridge, where you can pause to watch the creek or look at the mountaintops visible in all directions. Crushed rock at the far side of the bridge hints of future extension, but the trail becomes a narrow dirt tread filled with rocks and roots within 10 to 15 feet of the bridge. On the return, keep an eye out on your right after you reach the area of smaller trees for a good look at Vasilki Ridge.

A word of caution: There is no safety barrier on the downslope side of the trail, and even though the trail is paved, there are some steep areas. Assistance may be necessary.

32
BLACKPINE LAKE

Accessibility:	Easy
Distance:	0.5 mile round trip
Gradient:	Flat
Surface:	Pavement
When to go:	May–October
Parking:	Usable
Restrooms:	Yes (but the trail to the restroom is steep)
Information:	USFS Twisp District, (509) 997-2131

As you follow the shores of this sparkling, trout-filled lake, keep an eye and an ear alert for one of the beavers living in the area. The lucky few will see one of the buck-toothed beasts, but most will simply hear a splash as a beaver dives to safety or a loud, liquid "SLAP" as a sentry pounds its paddle-shaped tail against the lake surface, sounding the warning that humans are present.

The wide, level trail arcs around the edge of this kettle-shaped

Hoodoo Peak from Blackpine Lake (Photo: USFS, Methow Valley Ranger District)

tarn, formed when an ice block left by a glacier subsequently melted, leaving the depression that now holds the lake. In addition to the beavers that thrive around the lake and surrounding creeks, trout inhabit the lake, and the fishing is quite good. Although neither of the fishing piers are accessible, you may be able to cast from the shoreline trail.

A log curb forms a protective barrier on the trail's downhill side. Following the lakeshore for most of its length, the trail enters a forest before ending at a viewpoint over the valley and, looming above, the splendid Hoodoo Peak in the Lake Chelan-Sawtooth Wilderness.

From Twisp, take Twisp River Road west 10.6 miles, then turn left on Forest Road 43 (Buttermilk Creek Road). In 0.2 mile, the road forks. Stay left. In another 0.5 mile, Road 43 turns right. The pavement ends 4 miles after leaving Twisp River Road. Drive 2.5 miles from the end of the pavement, then bear left at the fork. The campground entrance is 0.7 mile after the intersection. The trailhead is located in the day use/dock area. It follows the north side of the lake to a viewpoint.

33
SIERRA PARK
FOR THE BLIND

Accessibility:	Easy
Distance:	0.25 mile loop
Gradient:	Generally flat
Surface:	Pavement and boardwalk
When to go:	All year
Parking:	Designated
Restrooms:	Yes
Information:	Edmonds Parks and Recreation, (206) 771-0220

This park delights all visitors. The trail through the park is landscaped with trees and shrubs, providing a wide range of textures and fragrances as well as visual beauty.

Interpretive sign, Sierra Park for the Blind

Visitors are encouraged to feel the difference in leaves, needles, and bark, as well as to enjoy the scents of herbs, aromatic shrubs, and trees. An alpine garden has been fashioned out of a rock outcrop. Picnic tables and wooden benches are located along pathways so you can linger along the trail.

Found within the city of Edmonds, Sierra Park is located at the intersection of 80th Avenue West and 190th Street Southwest. It is open daily from dawn to dusk.

The park and trail were designed and created through a partnership between the City of Edmonds and the Edmonds Lions Club.

34

🅔 🌷☀🍂❄

BURKE-GILMAN AND SAMMAMISH RIVER TRAILS

Accessibility: Easy
Distance: 54 miles round trip (many access/exit points)
Gradient: Generally flat, from 2% to 5%, one 20-yard hill to 15%
Surface: Pavement and some boardwalk
When to go: All year
Parking: Designated (at major parks along the trail)
Restrooms: Yes (a few are sporadically spaced along the way)
Information: King County Parks and Recreation, (206) 296-4232

The Burke-Gilman and Sammamish River trails are wonderful scenic corridors leading from Lake Union, past the northern tip of Lake Washington, to Marymoor Park in Redmond. These trails carry joggers, roller-bladers, bicyclists, walkers, and wheelchair users through urban and suburban Seattle. A word of caution: Although the cities have posted a 15 miles-per-hour speed limit, there's been little enforcement, so beware the occasional rampaging cyclist or roller-blader!

The Burke-Gilman and Sammamish River trails can be accessed at many points.

Four convenient spots are (1) near the end of the trail at Gas Works Park on Lake Union; (2) Matthews Beach Park near Northeast 93rd Street; (3) where the Burke-Gilman connects to the Sammamish River Trail at Log Boom Park, near the north end of Lake Washington; and (4) where the Sammamish River Trail ends at Marymoor Park in Redmond. Call the City of Seattle or King County Parks and Recreation to obtain a detailed map.

Near Gas Works Park on Lake Union, the trail's southernmost stretches offer views across blue waters to the city skyline, sailboats, and houseboats. Crossing the University of Washington campus, the path courses north between forested borders that separate it from Seattle residences, pausing at Lake Washington's Matthews

Burke-Gilman Trail

Beach Park. Northward for 5 miles, you are treated to views of Lake Washington and the Cascade Mountains beyond.

Just past Log Boom Park, the trail's underpass of a busy intersection is known to users as the "missing link"; it was completed in 1993, and allows users to connect easily with the Sammamish River Trail. From here the trail begins to feel more rural, running along the banks of the Sammamish Slough. Just beyond the golf course and through the tunnel, you head down a 20-yard, 15 percent grade. The trail then crosses over the slough and meanders towards

Woodinville. An exercise trail lines the pathway for approximately 5 miles from this point.

The trail winds through farmland and near several points of interest. These include the Bothell Landing Historic Park and Museum in Bothell and the Chateau Ste. Michelle and Columbia River wineries in Woodinville. Several King County parks are also near the trail, including Gold Creek Park, East Norway Hill Park, and Sixty Acres Park.

The trail ends at Marymoor Park. For more information on this 350-acre site, see the Marymoor Interpretive Trail description (trail 42).

35
SNOHOMISH CENTENNIAL TRAIL

E 🌷☀️🍂❄️

Accessibility:	Easy
Distance:	14 miles round trip (various entrance/exit points)
Gradient:	To 5%
Surface:	Pavement
When to go:	All year
Parking:	Designated
Restrooms:	Yes
Information:	Snohomish County Parks, (206) 388-6621

A wide, paved trail offers visitors a chance to enjoy a rural environment in a wide, fertile valley. This Rails to Trails conversion has been a favorite of trail users from the start. The 12-foot-wide paved Centennial Trail is paralleled by a 6-foot-wide horse route. Snohomish County has completed approximately 7 miles of this excellent multi-use trail. Eventually, it will stretch 44 miles between Skagit and King counties.

From Seattle, drive north on Interstate 5 to exit 194. Take this exit and drive east through the town of Snohomish to the light at the intersection of Second and D streets. Turn east at the light and left at the next light onto Maple Street. There is a trailhead at Maple and Pine streets, but it is recommended to continue approximately

Snohomish Centennial Trail, Mount Pilchuck on the right

1.5 miles on Maple Street to the large, well-signed parking area. A wheelchair ramp and portable restroom are located at the south end of the parking area. A second trailhead and parking area are found 3.1 miles north on South Machias Road.

The rural atmosphere is especially appealing to urbanites of all ages. The trail passes through valley farmland as it follows the picturesque

Pilchuck River. You can catch glimpses of Mount Pilchuck along the way. The new growth of spring and the colors of fall are great to see, but the trail offers a delightful experience year-round.

36
YOUTH ON AGE

E 🌷☀🍃

Accessibility:	Easy
Distance:	0.3 mile
Gradient:	Generally to 5%, one short grade to 10%
Surface:	Pavement
When to go:	March–November
Parking:	Usable
Restrooms:	Yes (an outhouse with bars)
Information:	USFS Darrington Ranger District, (360) 436-1155

Looping through a multi-species ancient forest, this trail explores the green world hiding under the canopy of huge Douglas firs, Sitka spruce, and western hemlock. Throughout this area are trees from each of those species that have reached more than 200 feet in height during their 500 years of life. The oldest and biggest trees are designated with interpretive signs detailing their size, age, and species.

The massive trees are the early attention-getters, but after a long look up at the giants, one's attention is diverted to the greenery carpeting the forest floor. Sprinkled throughout the forest are the plants that lend their name to the trail. The piggy-back plant, or "youth on age," is seen everywhere in the region. The name comes from the plant's unique design—the plant's stems spring up through a lower layer of leaves to sprout new leaves. The stem then continues up through those to start a new layer, and so on. The new growth rides on the back of the older plant, so it is "youth on age."

Between these creative ground plants and the huge conifers is a mature grove of big-leaf maples. Springtime visitors will love the cool green shade created by the moss-laden maples, while autumn explorers are awed by the brilliantly contrasting colors of the maples and the evergreens.

From Granite Falls, drive 19 miles east on State Route 92 (the Mountain Loop Highway) to the Verlot Ranger Station, where you will want to pause to pick up a nature trail guide before continuing down the road to the trailhead. (There is parking on both sides of the highway at Verlot, but the ranger station is on the north side.) With your new trail guide in hand, continue east on State Route 92 for another 8 miles to the trailhead parking area, found just east of the Red Bridge Campground on the south side of the highway.

The trail parallels the south fork of the Stillaguamish River, providing great views of the cold, tumbling waters of the river. The original trail was partially destroyed by the 1980 floods, and a short spur of that old route ends abruptly high above the river, providing a stunning view of the river valley. The rerouted trail continues along the river's edge.

Note: Rather rustic barrier-free toilet facilities are available at the trailhead, but we recommend a stop at the Verlot Ranger Station, where accessible, state-of-the-art restrooms are available year-round.

37
IRON GOAT

Accessibility:	Moderate
Distance:	2.4 miles round trip
Gradient:	To 8%
Surface:	Gravel
When to go:	March–November
Parking:	Designated (deep gravel may require assistance)
Restrooms:	Yes
Information:	USFS Skykomish Ranger District, (360) 677-2414

Natural history and American history combine here to produce a memorable trail experience. The forest—pushed back by the Great Northern Railway 100 years ago—has patiently waited to reclaim this corridor. Human ingenuity carved a railroad into the steep, inhospitable mountain, and the mountain eventually forced the

Railroad tunnel on the Iron Goat Trail

humans to move the rails. This new trail explores both the human struggle to maintain a transportation corridor and nature's struggle to maintain itself.

The story of the Iron Goat began 100 years ago, when the Great Northern Railway finally crossed the Cascades at Stevens Pass, helping to open the Northwest for settlement and trade with the rest of the world. The name "Iron Goat" comes from the Great Northern Railway logo, which featured the Rocky Mountain goat. This goat can still be spotted in the Stevens Pass area.

The original railway route over Stevens Pass was an intricate set of switchbacks that limited trains to 600 tons. The first Cascade Tunnel bypassed the switchbacks in 1900. Snowsheds were added to protect the route, but winter travel was still a hazard. Trains were often stopped for days by winter storms.

In 1910 one of the worst rail accidents in the history of the nation occurred at the town of Wellington, perched above Tye Creek. A section of snow broke loose and crashed down Windy Mountain, sweeping two trains off the tracks and into the Tye Valley below. Nearly 100 lives were lost in the accident. This prompted more improvements, including a concrete snowshed at the site of the Wellington avalanche. The snowshed still stands today.

As rail traffic increased, the maintenance of the snowsheds became too expensive. In 1929 the "new" 8-mile Cascade Tunnel was completed. This is still used today by Burlington Northern Railroad. The opening of that tunnel made the old grade obsolete, and it was abandoned completely. This abandoned stretch of railway was converted into the Iron Goat Trail by the teamwork of many different groups around Washington, led by Volunteers for Outdoor Washington. The Iron Goat Trail is on the National Historic Register.

From Skykomish, follow US Highway 2 east to milepost 55. Turn north onto Forest Service Road 67 and after 2.3 miles, turn left onto Road 6710. The parking area is 1.4 miles up the road. The parking area has some deep gravel, but it is passable to wheelchair users with moderate mobility.

The trail is wide and pleasant, although it can be muddy well into late summer. A few areas are somewhat difficult, most notably at the end of the trail, where it is poorly packed. The trail is removed from road noise and has lovely views of the surrounding peaks. Side trails to the upper trail are not barrier-free; they have steps and steep grades. There are plans to extend the trail.

38
DECEPTION FALLS

Accessibility:	Moderate
Distance:	0.4 mile round trip
Gradient:	From 6% to 16%
Surface:	Pavement and gravel
When to go:	April–November
Parking:	Designated
Restrooms:	Yes
Information:	USFS Skykomish Ranger District, (360) 677-2414

You can tell you're at the right trailhead by the thunderous roar of water that reverberates across the parking area. An information kiosk marks the start of the trail. The first part of the trail is

Trail bridge and highway bridge above Deception Falls

pavement and leads through moderate woods to a viewpoint of the upper falls. Pause here to enjoy a long, dry view of the falls, then travel over the crashing white water by way of an impressive steel arch bridge. The bridge's grated deck offers an exciting view of the water below. Prepare to get wet as you view the falls here: when the water is running high, spray mists up over visitors on the bridge.

Despite the dousing, though, this is the best view of the fast-moving stream as it falls under the highway bridge. Past the bridge, the accessible portion of the trail dead-ends at stone steps leading to a trail above the falls and on a somewhat steep grade under the highway.

A second, lower trail starts at a point halfway down the accessible portion of the trail. This trail was not intended to be barrier-free, and we rated it difficult to access. It starts with an uneven lip that drops off from the pavement to a narrow gravel trail with a steep grade of 20 percent. It leads to the lower falls and the swift Tye River.

From Monroe, drive east on State Route 2 through Skykomish. Deception Falls is on the north side of the highway, 8 miles east of Skykomish near milepost 56. Look for the sign.

39
CONFLUENCE AND WENATCHEE RIVERFRONT PARKS

Accessibility:	Easy
Distance:	10 miles round trip (various access/exit points)
Gradient:	Flat, with short parts to 8%
Surface:	Pavement
When to go:	February–November
Parking:	Designated
Restrooms:	Yes
Information:	Washington State Parks, (360) 902-8563

Those in search of the sun and big-sky country will love this trail. The wet forests are visible on the western horizon, but this is dry,

Confluence State Park and the Columbia River

arid country. You'll find great views of the Columbia River Valley and mountains to the west. The trail goes both north and south from Confluence State Park. At the time of our visit, the trail ended at the bridge north of the park. However, by the time you read this, the trail should extend over the Columbia and along the east bank, making a loop trip possible.

From Wenatchee take State Route 2 east toward the Columbia River, and just before crossing the bridge, turn south on State Route 97. The street descends into Confluence State Park. Before entering the park there, you will find a small parking area next to the trail. Inside the park there is additional parking as well as short trails leading to the main trail, which skirts the western boundary of the park.

Following our route south, cross the Wenatchee River on the bridge at the southwest corner of the park. Immediately after crossing the bridge is a wetland, with an inaccessible trail through it. The accessible trail continues above, with two turnouts and benches overlooking the wetland. Leaving the wetland, you enter an industrial area and eventually encounter a street. Turn left onto the sidewalk and continue 0.25 mile to where Hawley Street becomes North Miller Street. The sidewalk is cut and accessible. At the Hawley and North Miller intersection, the trail reappears on the left and gradually descends to the edge of the river. At Walla Walla Point, Confluence State Park ends and the trail enters the City of Wenatchee's Riverfront Park near some athletic fields.

Smell the cottonwoods lining the riverbank here! A sculpture honoring a native American fable titled *Coyote Leading the Salmon up the River* marks a moderately accessible gravel spur trail. It leads to a peninsula guarding a swimming area that is not accessible. Beyond here, the main trail becomes more rolling. There are restrooms and parking at Walla Walla Point, which can be reached in a car by turning from Wenatchee Avenue onto 9th Street. The views here are of the Stuart Range and Mission Ridge to the west. A sign also describes Wenatchee's early history, from its beginnings as a Hudson Bay outpost and native settlements near Confluence. At the south end of the park are more restrooms and an old log building. Beyond this building is a steeper descent, as the trail crosses a small stream.

The trail enters the Linden Tree Area through a delightful cottonwood grove. Note that several trees have deep notches cut by beavers. This area can also be reached in a car from 9th Street, where there is designated parking and more restrooms. Finally you will arrive at the old Steamboat Landing area with road access at 5th Street. The Waterfront Park ends at the Cascadian Fruit Storage plant, although a wide sidewalk continues to the pedestrian bridge, which is accessible, with a steep 12% grade. The bridge crosses the Columbia, but the views here are very limited, and the trail is in an industrial area. When the loop is completed, you may find more incentive to continue your explorations here.

40
WASHINGTON PARK ARBORETUM

Accessibility: Moderate to difficult
Distance: 2 mile network (various access/exit points)
Gradient: Moderate, with hills on some trails from 8% to 25%
Surface: Gravel and dirt
When to go: All year (rain may make areas impassable for wheelchairs)
Parking: Designated
Restrooms: Yes (at Graham Visitor Center)
Information: University of Washington Arboretum, (206) 543-8800

This is a great in-city getaway. This park is beautiful year-round, and you can learn about many plants from the terrific interpretive plaques. Unfortunately, the Arboretum is also frustrating. It was not designed with barrier-free access in mind, and the poor maintenance of trails does not help its accessibility. We strongly recommend that you have assistance the first time you explore these trails. If the weather is dry and the grass has been mowed, you may find many lawns, meadows, and trails negotiable. However, damp conditions persist here, and the mud can often be thick; this is not a place for thin tires!

From Seattle, drive east on State Route 520 and leave the highway via the Lake Washington Boulevard exit. Follow signs to the Arboretum and then to the Graham Visitor Center. Stop at the center to get maps, interpretive brochures, and information from the helpful volunteers.

Azalea Way is a 0.75-mile grassy thoroughfare in the heart of the Arboretum. Bordered by cherries, rhododendrons, and of course azaleas, this path is a great spring venture, although the ground can be damp. From here, a network of trails explores the upper hillside. Near the Woodland Garden, the trails are blocked by stairs. At the far end, you can either retrace your path, brave the network of trails, or take to Lake Washington Boulevard, which does not have much

Washington Park Arboretum

of a shoulder. If you turn left onto the road, you will reach the entrance to Arboretum Drive East in about half a block. Here you can use the pavement or venture again into the network of trails. From atop the hill, these trails may prove slightly more accessible.

You can most easily access the Foster Island trail from below the Broadmoor Golf Club entrance. The trailhead is steep and rutted from runoff, but shortly you are beside Duck Bay and then over an arched bridge. Watch for the antics of ducks and canoeists! Continuing onto Foster Island, you meander through meadows and large groves of trees and beneath State Route 520. Under the bridge it is muddy, but on the other side is a sunny knoll popular with picnickers. Having explored this meadow and the views of the lake and the Montlake Cut, you may wish to explore the accessible portion of the Waterfront Trail. This ends at a frustrating step-up onto the floating bridges. Still, you are in thick marsh brush for a few minutes.

The Japanese Garden is located on the opposite side of Lake Washington Boulevard. It is open from 10:00 A.M. all week, March 1 through November 30. There is a small admission fee. This garden represents a compressed world of mountains, forests, lakes, rivers, tablelands, and village. Pathways here are surfaced in gravel. Unfortunately, the stone bridges, stepping-stones, and rough terrain necessary for authentic landscaping are inaccessible. Still, there is much to be admired from several accessible vantage points.

41

COULON BEACH

Accessibility:	Easy
Distance:	3 miles round trip
Gradient:	From 2% to 6%
Surface:	Pavement and boardwalk
When to go:	All year
Parking:	Designated
Restrooms:	Yes
Information:	Renton Parks Department, (206) 235-2568

Tucked down on the Lake Washington waterfront in Renton are the hidden treasures of Coulon Beach Park. This park boasts many features, and using the accessible pathway stretching from end to end, you can uncover most of them. This accessible trail offers a perfect outdoor experience without leaving the shores of Seattle's suburbs.

From Bellevue, drive south on Interstate 405 and take the North 30th Street exit. Bear right at the end of the ramp. The road then veers left along the waterfront. The park is on your right-hand side, approximately 3 miles south on Lake Washington Boulevard East.

It's easy to find the trail from the accessible parking spaces located in the southern parking lot. Head around the southern beach swimming area to the Nature Island Bird Sanctuary Feeding

Area. Here you might be lucky enough to see goldeneye and common merganser ducks paddling through the cattails. Back over the John's Creek bridge, travel past the marina and Restaurant Pavilion. A floating dock reaches around the inner lagoon with two picnic floats, which are limited in accessibility. Just beyond the picnic area and past the large tulip tree, ducks and geese come in for slow-motion landings in the Log Boom pond. Marsh grass isolates the path as it meanders along Lake Washington's shore.

Highlights of this park include a short boardwalk and viewing platforms. Fishing is an option; a little luck might even bring in a bass, a squawfish, or a coveted salmon. The marshy waterways are home of red-winged blackbirds, leaping amid marsh grass and up into the larch trees at any notice of danger. The path leaves the hub of the park and travels parallel to an old railroad log-dump track. Mercer Island's shores provide a dramatic view to the northwest for the entire 1.5 miles.

42
MARYMOOR INTERPRETIVE TRAIL

Accessibility: Easy
Distance: 3 miles round trip
Gradient: Generally flat, from 2% to 5%
Surface: Dirt
When to go: All year
Parking: Designated
Restrooms: Yes
Information: King County Parks, Marymoor Park, (206) 296-2966

At the turn of the century, the 350-acre site now known as Marymoor Park was an internationally known farm called Willowmoor. It was not until 1940, when the Willowmoor Farm was sold a second time, that it was renamed "Marymoor" after the new owner's daughter.

In 1964 King County purchased the farm and began development of Marymoor as a regional park. Today, Marymoor boasts 524 acres, 17 soccer fields, 5 softball fields, a radio-controlled model aircraft area, 4 tennis courts, a bicycle velodrome, a community garden, and an accessible interpretive trail.

This trail circles the perimeter of the park, treating you to wetlands, lake views, and the winding slough. Interpretive signs along the way tell you about local plant and bird life. The compact dirt path climbs gently with grades ranging from 2 to 6 percent. The path narrows in a few locations, but it remains moderately accessible.

From Bellevue, drive east on State Route 520 and take the Marymoor exit. Turn right, then immediately left into the park.

This park is the center of much activity and affords you an invigorating snapshot of many of the outdoor recreational opportunities in our own backyards. Even as solely a trail user, you can partake of many activities at Marymoor. Picnic shelters are available for reservation, while the Cline Mansion and the Marymoor Museum sport an interesting collection of facts and artifacts. The park also hosts annual events, including the Heritage Festival on the Fourth of July weekend. If you are looking to "get out of the house" and enjoy the outdoors, Marymoor Park will suit you perfectly.

43
TRADITION LAKES

Accessibility: Easy (except for steep access)
Distance: 0.6 mile round trip
Gradient: To 6%
Surface: Boardwalk
When to go: All year
Parking: Usable
Restrooms: Yes
Information: DNR Enumclaw, (360) 825-1631

Waterfowl lovers will love this trail; it leads through a quiet, lush forest before reaching an overlook of a small lake frequented by migratory ducks and geese—some of which spend the winter and stay to nest in the spring.

As you start up the trail, you are immersed in the quiet of a dense forest. The trail winds through the trees and varied undergrowth, including huckleberry, salal, and ferns, before breaking out above the lovely lake that appears well below the trail. Providing a back-drop for the sparkling water are the tree-lined Cascade foothills. Beyond the lake, the trail becomes inaccessible—too narrow, rough, and steep for those with mobility limitations. Though it is a short trip, this trail is worth a visit. It provides a perfect alpine lake experience in the lowlands. It is understandable why the area is locally referred to as the Issaquah Alps.

From Seattle, drive east on Interstate 90 to exit 20. Take this exit and, at the bottom of the ramp, turn right onto the short road leading to the parking area. Actually, the entire road is used for parking. After parking your vehicle, follow Puget Power Road, which is quite steep (well over 8 percent in places) to the actual trailhead.

If you call several days in advance, a Department of Natural

Trail around Tradition Lakes (Photo: Susan Combs-Bauer)

Resources employee will meet you at the gated Puget Power Access Road so that you may drive to a parking spot beyond the steep grade.

44

Ⓜ 🌷☀🍂❄

SNOQUALMIE RIVER

Accessibility: Moderate
Distance: Spring Glen Road to Tokul Tunnel, 6 miles round trip; Nick Loutsis Park to missing trestle at Spring Glen Road, 12.8 miles round trip; Nick Loutsis Park to first unimproved trestle before Duvall, 11.4 miles round trip
Gradient: Generally low, with gradual elevation changes
Surface: Gravel
When to go: All year
Parking: Usable
Restrooms: No
Information: King County Parks, (206) 296-4151

Once a branch of the Milwaukee Railroad, this trail holds great promise for the future. Right now trail access and conditions are a little rough, but King County Parks will continue to make improvements as funding is available.

In that context, the highlight of this trail is the stretch from Spring Glen Road to Tokul Tunnel. At the time of this writing there was no access to and from the trail at Tokul Tunnel, and past the tunnel the trail was inaccessible. Additionally, at the time of our visit, trail access was virtually blocked at Spring Glen Road by a 3-foot-high mound of dirt. King County Parks has promised to remove this mound, so presumably it won't be a problem by the time you read these words, but take this note as our exemption from blame should the mound remain at the time of your visit.

With those cautions in mind, this is a gorgeous rural route. With views down into the Snoqualmie Valley, this trail is surrounded by trees and fields. A spectacular curving bridge high above the white water of Tokul Creek will draw your "oohs" and "aahs."

To reach the small parking area at Spring Glen Road, from Seattle, follow Interstate 90 east to State Route 203 (Preston/Fall City/Snoqualmie Road Southeast). Follow this north through Fall City, and at 2 miles past Fall City, turn left (east). Continue for 0.7 mile to the trail.

To reach Nick Loutsis Park, continue north on State Route 203 to downtown Carnation, take Entwhistle Road east, and drive 4 blocks to Milwaukee Avenue. This is the site of the old Carnation train station.

Easiest, and assured, access may be obtained at Nick Loutsis Park in Carnation. And, by the time you read these words, it should be possible for you to follow the trail from the park all the way to Tokul Tunnel. King County Parks now has the funding to rebuild the only missing trestle between the park and the tunnel, making for a very long day hike!

In any case, the park gives access to two long sections of trail, with trees overhead, fields below, views of the valley, birds, the sound of streams, and the company of walkers, cyclists, and horseback riders. The autumn should bring spectacular colors to the many deciduous trees along the trail.

45
CREEKSIDE LOOP AT MOUNT SI

Accessibility: Easy
Distance: 500 feet
Gradient: Less than 5%
Surface: Packed gravel
When to go: All year
Parking: Designated
Restrooms: Yes
Information: DNR Enumclaw, (360) 825-1631

Wrapped around a forest meadow at the base of Mount Si, this trail provides an easy exploration of the meadow and forest environments. Unlike much of the western Cascades, the forest here is largely deciduous, with huge big-leaf maple and alder trees the most common species, although there are a few old oaks and smaller vine maples.

The firmly packed gravel loop trail offers two picturesque log bridges over the frog- and crawfish-filled stream. For those wanting to picnic here, there are five tables spaced around the meadow. For the casual traveler, benches are scattered along the route for rest and reflection.

While the scenery is beautiful, most visitors find it hard to avoid being distracted from the natural wonders by the stream of humanity rushing up Mount Si. The Creekside Loop Trail provides a great view of the main Mount Si trail, and on any given day you may see anything from a wedding party in formal wear to fitness fanatics running up the steep mountain wearing little more than running shoes.

Peeled-log bridge at Mount Si (Photo: Susan Combs-Bauer)

From Seattle, take Interstate 90 east to exit 31 at North Bend. Drive into town and continue east on North Bend Way. One mile after leaving the city limits, turn left on Mount Si Road and drive 2.5 miles to a packed dirt and gravel parking lot on the left. Designated parking is available on the far end of the parking area, closest to the trailhead.

46
M ⚘ ☀ 🌿

TINKHAM DISCOVERY

Accessibility:	Moderate
Distance:	0.5 mile round trip
Gradient:	Generally flat, to 8%
Surface:	Gravel
When to go:	April–October
Parking:	Usable
Restrooms:	Yes (in campground)
Information:	USFS North Bend District, (206) 888-1421

Here's a chance to discover the amazing ability of a forest to rebound from a loss. This second-growth forest was logged several decades ago, but all that remains of that period are a few lingering stumps. Even the stumps have played a role in the new forest, however. Just as fallen trees act as nursemaids to new sprouts in old-growth forests, here the dead stumps have proven to be fertile ground for new growth.

At the beginning of summer, 1995, the first 0.25 mile of the trail had been completed. Winding through second-growth forest, the trail was not accessible past a cedar boardwalk. The numerous huge old stumps—many still showing the springboard notches used by the loggers—are scattered throughout the second-growth forest. Taking a closer look at several of the tall, young trees reveals that their roots are firmly planted in the flat tops of decaying stumps; in essence, the new trees have nursed sustenance out of the old, dead husks.

From Seattle, follow Interstate 90 to exit 42. Take this exit, drive southeast 1.5 miles to the Tinkham Creek Campground, and continue along the one-way campground loop to the far east end, where the road turns north. The trailhead is found in the Tinkham Creek Campground.

To the north of the trail is a stream that has been blocked by a beaver dam upstream. When built, the remainder of the trail will eventually circle the beaver pond, crossing the inlet stream by boardwalk. Look for signs of the historic wagon road over the pass—some of its boardwalk is visible from the trail.

Volunteer labor built this trail, which was funded in part by the clearing and timber sale on land adjacent to the campground. This trail offers a pleasant walk in the woods even now, but when completed, the trail will be outstanding. Accessible restrooms and picnic tables are located along the road that divides the campground in half.

47
GOLD CREEK POND

Accessibility:	Easy
Distance:	1 mile round trip
Gradient:	Generally flat, to 8%
Surface:	Pavement
When to go:	May–October
Parking:	Designated
Restrooms:	No
Information:	USFS North Bend District, (206) 888-1421

Surrounded by the tall, craggy peaks of the Alpine Lakes Wilderness, this trail offers a wonderful opportunity to marvel at the mighty Cascades. The wide, paved trail leaves the parking area and dips to a small pond—a perfect reflecting pool for the surrounding mountains.

From Seattle, drive east on Interstate 90 to exit 54, signed Hyak/Gold Creek. Take this exit, and at the end of the off-ramp, turn left (north). The paved road immediately turns right (east). Continue approximately 1 mile, then turn left (north) on a dirt road signed Gold Creek. In 0.4 mile, bear left at the fork in the road and enter a large gravel general parking area. The paved, accessible parking is on the north edge of the gravel area.

An asphalt trail leads from the parking area west toward a pond, which is a gravel pit that filled with water following the construction of Interstate 90. The trail crosses the outlet from the pond and comes to a picnic area. From here the views up the Gold Creek Valley are magnificent. At the head of the valley are Huckleberry and Chikamin peaks; to the west Kendall Peak, and to the east Rampart Ridge. This view and its reflection on the pond are enough to make this trip outstanding.

The area around the pond is open and sunny in summer, making it a great picnic getaway from the roar of Interstate 90. As you leave the picnic area, the trail runs between the pond and Gold Creek to the west, eventually winding around and descending to the pond. Interpretive displays at log-rimmed viewpoints with benches provide additional information about the area. The site has been extensively replanted, and the small trees are just visible along the trail. There is no accessible fishing at this site. The north end of the pond borders private land that is being developed.

48
LAKE KACHESS

M ❧ ☀ ❦

Accessibility:	Moderate
Distance:	0.5 mile loop
Gradient:	Generally flat, stretches to 10%
Surface:	Dirt and gravel
When to go:	April–October
Parking:	Usable
Restrooms:	Yes
Information:	USFS Cle Elum District, (509) 674-4411

This is a wonderful trail that follows and crosses the tumbling waters of Box Canyon Creek before entering a century-old second-growth forest. The trail winds up at an overlook with pretty views of the lake and, beyond that, Thorpe Mountain. Look closely to see the old fire lookout tower at Thorpe's summit.

From Seattle, follow Interstate 90 and take exit 62, signed Stampede Pass/Lake Kachess, and continue north along the paved road (which eventually becomes Forest Service Road 49) for 5 miles to a three-way intersection. Take a right at the intersection and enter the Kachess Campground. Beyond the entrance pay station at

Big trees in the Kachess Campground

0.1 mile, you come to another intersection. Stay left and follow this road about 0.5 mile to the parking area for Little Kachess Trail No. 1312. A little farther beyond this trailhead is an additional parking area that allows you to avoid the first part of the trail, which is uphill.

The trail is on packed dirt with an overlay of up to 1 inch of coarse gravel. The coarseness of the surface may prove difficult for thin wheels, so assistance may be required. After a short distance, the trail crosses the pretty little stream on a bridge built by the Student Conservation Association, a group providing opportunities for high school and college students to work in natural resource areas. The trail then climbs to a bench above the lake. The viewing area overlooks the creek and the campground.

From this point, the trail loops to another broad rest area with views of the lake. To make the most of the viewpoint, relax in an easy chair carved from a tree stump and partake of the scenery before you—the glistening lake, the densely forested hills, and looming Thorpe Mountain.

The return portion of the loop travels next to a huge moss-covered rock slab with several large trees growing out of the rock. The forest is very beautiful, with trees that are 80 to 100 years old. This is a truly enjoyable trail.

SOUTH
CASCADES

49
WOODARD BAY TRAIL

Accessibility: Paved part easy, unpaved part difficult
Distance: Paved part 4 miles, entire trail 12 miles round trip
Gradient: Flat
Surface: Pavement and railroad ballast (rough in spots)
When to go: All year
Parking: Usable
Restrooms: No
Information: DNR Chehalis, (360) 753-3410

Like Seattle's Burke-Gilman Trail, this trail traverses the backyards of industry, city, suburbs, farms, and woods. The northern section of trail is the most secluded, but the area that is currently paved is also delightful.

Unfortunately, the pavement ends where the best scenery begins. In dry weather there is good incentive to bring along a strong assistant to help explore the unpaved reaches of the trail. Here you travel beneath beautiful shade trees and beside pastures, ponds, and farmyards. You are likely to see a wide variety of birds as well as the occasional deer, coyote, possum, squirrel, or raccoon.

There are no amenities or telephones on this portion of trail, and road crossings are few and far between.

From Seattle, drive south on Interstate 5 to exit 105B (marked as the Port of Olympia). From the off-ramp, merge right onto Plum Street and continue through Olympia, where the street name changes to East Bay Drive. At 2.6 miles, it changes again to Boston Harbor Road. When you reach the fork at 6.2 miles, veer right onto Woodard Bay Road. At 7.3 miles, this road merges onto Libby Road. Take the first (almost immediate) right in order to continue on Woodard Bay Road. At 7.9 miles, on the left side of the road and immediately before the small bridge over Woodard Bay, is the unsigned gravel parking area.

Big Creek Falls (Trail no. 73)

Woodard Bay

50
WOODARD BAY
CONSERVATION AREA

Accessibility: Easy
Distance: 1.2 miles round trip
Gradient: Generally flat, one part to 8%
Surface: Pavement
When to go: All year
Parking: Usable
Restrooms: No
Information: DNR Chehalis, (360) 753-3410

Pass through the conservation area gates and you can wander through the lush woodlands that border Woodard Bay, a small tidal inlet popular with harbor seals, fish, and more than 100 species of upland birds and waterfowl.

From Seattle, drive south on Interstate 5 to exit 105B (marked as the Port of Olympia). From the off-ramp, merge right onto Plum Street and continue through Olympia, where the street name changes to East Bay Drive. At 2.6 miles, it changes again to Boston Harbor Road. When you reach the fork at 6.2 miles, veer right onto Woodard Bay Road. At 7.3 miles, this road merges onto Libby Road. Take the first (almost immediate) right in order to continue on Woodard Bay Road. At 7.9 miles, on the left side of the road and immediately before the small bridge over Woodard Bay, is the unsigned gravel parking area.

From there, a gated access road leads out into the conservation area. Blocked to all but authorized vehicles, this paved road makes for a very enjoyable barrier-free stroll. The road, which rises over a gradual hill, offers good views of the shoreline and wildlife. In the evenings, look for bats; a large colony lives nearby.

At the end of your journey, enjoy a meal and rest at picnic tables just above the tidal zone. Here you can see the abandoned railway dock and appreciate this former industrial site's return to nature. This is a prime example of environmental restoration.

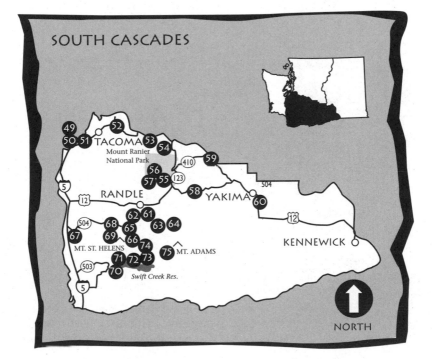

The area was one of the first sites purchased after the Natural Resources Conservation Areas (NRCA) program was created in 1987. Originally owned by Weyerhaeuser, this NRCA consists of 282 upland acres and 190 tideland acres.

Prior to white settlement of the area, the 1,800 members of the Nisqually Tribe used the area around Woodard and Chapman bays for gathering shellfish and as protection from raiding parties. In 1853 Harvey Rice Woodard became the first permanent white settler with his 320-acre land claim.

From 1924 to 1928, Weyerhaeuser purchased and developed the land for a log dump and the right-of-way for the Chehalis Western Railroad. The log dump served as a crucial link between company's 211,000 acres of timberlands in southwest Washington and its sawmills in Everett. Over nearly sixty years, approximately 14.8 billion board feet of logs moved through the Woodard Bay log storage. At peak capacity, in one day 120 or more carloads of logs (about 1 million board feet) were unloaded, sorted, and rafted. Each week two to three log rafts with 700,000 board feet left the site for the Everett sawmills.

51
NISQUALLY NATIONAL WILDLIFE REFUGE

Accessibility: Moderate
Distance: 1 mile loop and 5.5 mile loop
Gradient: Generally flat, ramps 6% to 20%
Surface: Dirt and gravel
When to go: All year
Parking: Usable (loose, thick gravel may require assistance)
Restrooms: Yes
Information: Nisqually National Wildlife Refuge, (360) 753-9467

The Nisqually River Delta is known among bird watchers as the place to go to see waterfowl and shorebirds. The delta is one of the last undisturbed estuaries along the shores of Puget Sound, and therefore attracts a multitude of native and migratory birds. These trails travel past both freshwater and saltwater wetlands, as well as through beautiful woodlands. The refuge is a wonderful experience, with beautiful sites in all weather. Be aware that areas of the trail may be muddy or slick when wet.

From Seattle, drive south on Interstate 5 to exit 114, signed Nisqually/Old Nisqually and found just after crossing the Nisqually River Bridge. Take the exit and follow the signs 0.4 mile to the entrance of the refuge parking area. The parking area and route to the trails is covered with loose gravel, up to 1 inch deep, which may prove difficult for those without assistance or with thin wheels.

Trail and wildlife information are available at the trailhead kiosk.

Spring-fed pond, Nisqually Wildlife Refuge

Tidal marsh, Nisqually Wildlife Refuge

The Twin Barn Loop is 1 mile. It leads to the Twin Barn Education Center, with exhibits about the refuge. The center is open on weekends, 10 A.M. to 3 P.M. The portion of the loop that connects the Twin Barns to the Brown Farm Dike Trail consists of a raised boardwalk, with steep earthen ramps at each end. These ramps have 6 to 20 percent grades and may require assistance to negotiate.

The Brown Farm Dike Trail is 5.5 miles. It is generally flat, but can often be muddy. On the trail, which follows the Nisqually River, the Nisqually Reach, and McAllister Creek, you can catch beautiful views of these waters and the diverse wildlife sheltered by the refuge.

52
WEST HYLEBOS WETLANDS

Accessibility:	Easy
Distance:	1 mile loop
Gradient:	To 3%
Surface:	Boardwalk and gravel
When to go:	All year
Parking:	Usable
Restrooms:	No
Information:	Dash Point State Park, (206) 593-2206

This gem is well worth a visit to the southern realms of Federal Way. In the heart of new development, this 60-acre wetland delights everyone. Follow the well-groomed path past a fine old maple tree that cradles a bird-nesting box. From here on you encounter detailed interpretive signs, beginning with two carefully written markers, offering photos and names of surrounding plants along with a history of their uses.

The path quickly turns into a boardwalk, taking you over the damp ground and enticing you to pause on the route's broad turnouts and rustic, comfortable benches. In addition to providing details on the flora and fauna of the region, the interpretive signs tell about the ecology and geology of wetlands. Particularly interesting are the remnants of an ancient lake, called "deep sinks."

As you continue on, you pass over still pools—listen for the tumble of water as well as for the sounds of wrens, frogs, and pileated woodpeckers. As you follow the trail, you are encouraged to enjoy the natural settings with all your senses—touch and smell the leaves, bark, and moss! Everything is within reach, even a fallen tree's huge trunk and root system. Wandering the paths, it isn't hard to imagine the terrible crashes that must result when wind-blown trees fall. The trees at West Hylebos are particularly susceptible to wind because the water table here is just below the surface and most of the trees are "floating" on shallow root systems. About halfway along the loop, a spur trail leads through the brush and over a broad streambed. At the end, enjoy the observation deck and bench overlooking tiny Brook Lake.

From Seattle, follow Interstate 5 south to exit 142. Take this exit and drive west on South 348th Street, cross Pacific Highway South, and at 1 mile, turn left onto 4th Avenue South. Be careful here—

Boardwalk at West Hylebos Wetlands (Photo: Marge and Ted Mueller)

this is a tiny, one-lane side street. There is a small power station just beyond it. Drive 2 blocks, and turn left into the gravel parking area. Maps are available at the trailhead kiosk.

West Hylebos State Park was created from purchases and donations of several smaller pieces of land. This outstanding park and nature trail are a credit to the hard work of local residents and community groups. Afterwards, when driving Interstate 5 south of Federal Way, remember to look for the West Hylebos Creek signs!

Note: Be aware that this is a raised boardwalk trail with no safety barriers on the edges. Caution is advised, especially if the boardwalk is wet.

53
FEDERATION FOREST

Accessibility: Moderate
Distance: 0.4 mile loop
Gradient: To 5%
Surface: Packed gravel and dirt
When to go: May–August
Parking: Designated
Restrooms: Yes
Information: Washington State Parks, (360) 902-8563

Prior to exploring this trail, spend some time in the Catherine Montgomery Interpretive Center. Of special interest are the center's living displays.

From Enumclaw, drive east for 17 miles on State Route 410 (the Chinook Pass Highway) to the Federation Forest State Park on the south side of the highway.

The trailhead is found on the north end of the building, at the Natural Trail sign. Be sure to follow the East Loop signs, as the west loop is somewhat narrow and much more difficult. This interpretive trail is located atop an ancient river terrace. On the trail, you

Federation Forest (Photo: Marge and Ted Mueller)

can hear the White River only a few feet below, but you never catch
a glimpse of it.

Portions of the trail narrow down to 3 feet, and tangled roots
crawl over some areas, but the grade never reaches above 5 percent.
Be sure to notice the "slowly falling tree" as you travel the trail,
and as you enjoy the beauty of the area, say a silent thank you to

Fred Cleator, a conservationist and forester who was instrumental in acquiring and preserving this area.

54
MUIR DISCOVERY

Ⓔ 🌱 ☀ 🌿

Accessibility:	Easy
Distance:	0.8 mile loop
Gradient:	Flat
Surface:	Pavement
When to go:	April–November
Parking:	Usable
Restrooms:	Yes
Information:	USFS White River District, (360) 825-6585

This is a classic example of a multi-aged forest. Young, brash alder continue to grow throughout the area, but those quick-growing deciduous trees are slowly being shadowed out by the older, taller hemlock and western red cedar conifers. Because of the diversity, the forest canopy is open just enough to allow for a lush, green carpet of moss all over the forest floor.

From Enumclaw, drive 24.6 miles east on State Route 410 to The Dalles Campground. The trailhead is within the campground. After entering the campground, continue straight into the picnic area. A covered picnicking facility is visible from the campground entrance—the trail begins here, at the left side of the parking area.

Although a kiosk was slated for construction, at the time of our visit the trailhead was not well marked. There are two ways to begin the trail. The easiest way is to stay left of the picnic pavilion and head toward the river.

The trail winds along the banks of the White River with at least a few good viewing areas before turning into the forest. Notice how the rushing water lives up to its name. The milky hue of the river is a result of the glacier silt—the dust-sized bits of rock ground up by the creeping glaciers—churned into the water. Occasional benches and interpretive signs dot the trail.

55

BOX CANYON
OF THE COWLITZ

Accessibility: Difficult
Distance: 0.25 mile
Gradient: Generally 7%, parts to 12%, one spot to 30%
Surface: Pavement
When to go: July–October
Parking: Designated
Restrooms: Yes
Information: Mount Rainier National Park, (360) 569-2211

Box Canyon is actually more of a slot than a box—a deep, narrow slot carved into the rock by the pounding white water of the Cowlitz River.

From Enumclaw, take State Route 410 to Cayuse Pass, then continue south on State Route 123 to the Stevens Canyon Road turnoff. Follow Stevens Canyon Road 10 miles to the parking area for Box Canyon of the Cowlitz. Follow the signs to the Overlook Bridge for the trailhead.

As you approach the Cowlitz on Stevens Canyon Road, you are treated to some wonderful vistas of Mount Rainier. You lose sight of the mountain once you come to the trail, but you find instead a nice, pleasant little valley. Your first indication that there is more to this valley than first meets the eye is the roar that comes from what appears to be a crease in the rocks ahead. As you draw closer to the edge and peer down, hang on to your hat—literally. A sheer drop of 180 feet to the plunging river greets the surprised first-time visitor to this canyon. When you look down into the canyon, you find that the depth of the fissure is enhanced by its narrowness. But the most impressive thing about the canyon is the river being funneled through the narrow slot. Fresh from the ice of the Cowlitz Glacier, the river slashes and pounds its way through the rock. Its potential power is apparent when you notice the huge logs wedged between the canyon walls some 20 to 30 feet above the

Glacial striation, a major feature of Box Canyon before the rock was leveled for a wayside exhibit

river—a sign that, as awesome as the normal flow is, the river at flood stage must be downright scary.

All this is visible from the 0.25-mile overlook trail, which is best visited starting from the easternmost trailhead, so that you travel the trail in a counterclockwise direction. The last half of the trail narrows, and obstacles appear more frequently. The paved trail curves gently through the meadows perched above the canyon.

The path is guided by guardrails all the way around and generally maintains a 7 percent slope. At the halfway point, the trail takes a very wide but extremely steep turn (30 percent grade), then crosses a bridge. The bridge affords an opportunity to look straight down all 120 feet into the roiling river. The last portion of the trail narrows to 3.5 and 4 feet, while obstacles such as rocks and roots are exposed. Be sure to visit the Wayside Exhibit across the street from the trailhead, where a 50-foot trail offers a perfect vantage point from which to gaze upon Mount Rainier and Mount Adams.

56
PARADISE LOOPS

Accessibility: Moderate to difficult
Distance: 0.1 mile to several miles
Gradient: From 7% to 15%
Surface: Pavement
When to go: July–November
Parking: Designated
Restrooms: Yes
Information: Mount Rainier National Park, (360) 569-2211

For unobstructed, unbeatable views of Mount Rainier, there is no place better than Paradise. Behind the Jackson Visitor Center in the Paradise Area is a network of meadow trails that take advantage of the views. The trails are all paved, but they vary in accessibility. The Nisqually Vista Trail and the Skyline Trail have the least grade and offer outlets to further trail explorations. Except

Henry Jackson Visitor Center at Mount Rainier

for the slightly steeper climb from the parking area up into the meadows, these two trails maintain steady 7 percent grades.

As the trail winds around meadow trees and passes natural benches, you catch outstanding views of Mount Rainier's grandeur.

Throughout the summer, alpine flowers paint the meadows in brilliant colors. By September colorful blooms are replaced by the crimson vines of ground-hugging blueberry bushes, offering a different— but equally beautiful—frame for views of the mountain. Don't forget, too, that by September the sweet, blue fruit on those bushes is ripe and delicious.

As you admire the mountain, look closely and you are likely to see summit expeditions on the Camp Muir Route (ask a ranger at Paradise to point out the route to you before you venture onto the trail, so you will know where to look). Traveling the Skyline Trail you encounter Myrtle Falls, and at some times of the year, you can see the ice caves at the distant base of the Nisqually Glacier. To get a better view of these wonders, bring your binoculars!

From Tacoma, drive east on State Route 7 to Elbe. Continue east on State Route 706 to the entrance of Mount Rainier National Park, and then continue for 16 miles to the parking area near the Jackson Visitor Center at Paradise.

The visitor center offers more information about Mount Rainier and local history.

57
TRAIL OF THE SHADOWS

Accessibility: Easy to difficult
Distance: 0.5 mile loop
Gradient: From 3% to 12%
Surface: Gravel and boardwalk
When to go: July–November
Parking: Designated
Restrooms: Yes
Information: Mount Rainier National Park, (360) 569-2211

This 0.5-mile loop takes you around a steaming marsh and through more than a century of history. A 20-acre area, long visited by local native tribes, became part of a mining claim established by the

Longmire family in 1887. The area was rich in minerals, and the Longmires mined magnesium, iron, and sodium chloride. They found that the true wealth of the site, though, was in the beauty of the surroundings.

From Tacoma, drive east on State Route 7 to Elbe. Continue east on State Route 706 to the entrance of Mount Rainier National Park, and continue 6 miles to Longmire. The trailhead is across the road from the Longmire Hotel. We recommend traveling the path in a counterclockwise direction (around the northern end first). In this direction, you encounter a gradual 8 percent grade. The trail flattens as you pass an old cabin dating from 1888. Continuing along the trail, you find proof that Mount Rainier is still an active volcano, should anyone doubt it: an acrid odor of sulfur lingers around several steaming ponds and marshes, evidence of the fiery cauldron still simmering just below the surface. For now, though, the mountain is calm—no need to worry about an eruption today.

Moving on, follow the trail as it loops around the west end of the marsh, where a few short piers let you visit with the water life. On this portion of the trail, watch for obstructing roots. The path begins and ends in gentle 3 percent grades.

58
CLEAR LAKE

Accessibility:	Easy
Distance:	1.2 miles round trip
Gradient:	Flat
Surface:	Pavement
When to go:	May–October
Parking:	Designated
Restrooms:	Yes
Information:	USFS Naches District, (509) 653-2205

On the western shore of Clear Lake, with great views of the high, surrounding ridges and peaks, this day-use area is fully wheelchair accessible. Here you can enjoy tables, barbecues, fireplaces, and restrooms that are completely barrier-free, and all in the shadow of the William O. Douglas Wilderness.

From Yakima, follow US Highway 12 to its junction with Tieton Reservoir Road (Forest Service Road 12), just east of White Pass. Turning onto Tieton Reservoir Road, travel 2.6 miles south to the facility entrance on the left side of the road.

The amenities include a community shelter and cooking area, a 1.2-mile round-trip interpretive trail, two wildlife-viewing blinds, two fishing platforms, and five individual picnic/cooking pads. The fishing platforms are on an approximately 250-foot lakefront trail that starts from the main trail with a very short, easy downslope. The platforms also have lower sections in the standard railing to accommodate fishing at wheelchair height. Potable water is not available.

59
BOULDER CAVE NO. 962A

Accessibility:	Easy
Distance:	0.75 mile loop
Gradient:	Flat
Surface:	Pavement
When to go:	April–October
Parking:	Designated
Restrooms:	Yes
Information:	USFS Naches District, (509) 653-2205

Catch the beauty of a mountain stream as you rest and enjoy the surroundings from carefully placed benches. This trail explores an area adjacent to the Naches River. The interpretive signs here are a pleasure, as they describe in detail the natural history of the region. Because the Naches is an excellent trout stream, it is likely that if you watch for a while, you will get a demonstration of fly-fishing as anglers move up the river, making their long, graceful casts over the blue water.

From Yakima, follow State Route 410 until you are about 7 miles east of Bumping River Road. Look for the large Old River Road/Camp Roganunda sign, which indicates where to turn for the bridge over the Naches River. Turn right just past the bridge, and continue on the paved road for 1 mile to the Boulder Cave parking area.

Boulder Cave Campground, located near the trailhead, offers a picnic area and reduced-service overnight camping. No water is available, except for treated water from the river, which must be treated. The trailhead for Boulder Cave Trail No. 962 is also located here.

60
YAKIMA GREENWAY

Accessibility: Easy
Distance: 14 miles round trip
Gradient: Generally flat, grades to 5%
Surface: Pavement
When to go: All year (except when snow- and ice-covered)
Parking: Designated
Restrooms: Yes
Information: Yakima Greenway Foundation, (509) 453-8280

This pathway offers a little of everything and so has something to offer everyone. From the trail you can explore the banks of the Yakima River, a major tributary of the Columbia River; view birds, including herons, ospreys, and a growing population of bald eagles; enjoy shady woods areas alive with cottontail rabbits; and make use of several boat landing areas scattered along the route. Benches and picnic tables with moderate accessibility are located at strategic locations along the trail, and fishing is available at numerous lakes passed by the route.

The Greenway path begins at Harlan Landing (in Selah Gap)

and ends at Valley Mall Boulevard (in Union Gap). The Greenway is accessible from all parks and landings except Century Landing. A map of the city may be helpful for those unfamiliar with the Yakima area.

The Greenway includes the Noel and Jewett pathways and offers access to the Yakima Arboretum. Here are some of the other notable features and access points of the Greenway:

Harlan Landing: Parking, boat ramp, bring-your-own-equipment volleyball court, picnic/barbecue and restroom facilities, and northern end of greenway. Exit Interstate 82 at Resthaven Road, and go west (over the freeway) into the parking area.

Rotary Lake: Access to sixteen parking and fishing piers designated for the disabled, restrooms, and picnic facilities. Go north on 4th Street, east on R Street, follow gravel road under freeway to parking area, and then go north on pathway 0.5 mile to lake.

Sarg Hubbard Park and Landing: Parking, river access, amphitheater, picnic/barbecue facilities (including US West Picnic Shelter, which may be reserved), play area, physical fitness course, viewing platforms (not accessible), and restrooms. Exit Interstate 82 at Terrace Heights Road, go east, and turn south on 18th Street. Just north of this park, along the trail route, is a large, fully accessible playground.

Sherman Park: Parking, Fred Westberg Memorial Picnic Pavilion (which may be reserved), nature trails, children's play area, and southern end of Noel Pathway. Enter from Nob Hill Boulevard across from Kmart.

Robertson Landing: Parking, boat ramp, picnic and restroom facilities, and northern end of Jewett Pathway. Enter from Nob Hill Boulevard at Sherman Park, and continue east past the Humane Society.

Jewett Pathway Parking: Restrooms, picnic facilities, and southern end of Jewett Pathway. Exit Interstate 82 at Valley Mall Boulevard and go east.

Natural Area: This area will remain largely undeveloped and protected.

Century Landing: Parking, boat ramp, and picnic/barbecue and restroom facilities on east side of river. Exit Interstate 82 at Thorpe Road (south of Union Gap), and drive north on Thorpe Road.

61
WOODS CREEK
WATCHABLE WILDLIFE

Accessibility: Moderate
Distance: Main trail 1.5 miles, old growth 1 mile
Gradient: Main trail to 8%, old growth to 12%
Surface: Gravel (old-growth loop may remain compacted dirt)
When to go: March–November
Parking: Designated
Restrooms: Yes
Information: USFS Randle District, (360) 497-7565

This is a great chance to witness the biological diversity found in a natural wetland! From beavers to black-tailed deer, from mosquitoes to mallards, this forest wetland is home to a vast list of wildlife species. With a little luck and patience, you can view many of the animals.

From Packwood, follow US Highway 12 west to Randle, and at the stoplight turn south on State Route 131. This highway becomes Forest Service Road 23/25. Cross the bridge just outside town, and at the next fork in the road, bear right. Follow Road 25 for 5 miles to the Woods Creek Information Center. The trailhead is directly across the road.

Trail guides from the kiosk correspond to interpretive markers along the trail, giving information about the area and its wildlife. Before heading out, though, be sure to slather on insect repellent, since the smallest of the wetland inhabitants, especially the mosquitoes and flies, are the most vicious and bloodthirsty.

The trail rolls through a dark, mixed hardwood and coniferous forest before leading across a meadow created by farmland-hungry homesteaders in the late 1800s. From the meadow, the main trail crosses a bridge spanning the wetlands.

Just before the bridge, a side trail leads away to the east. This

A swampy wide spot in Woods Creek

trail is a mile-long loop through old-growth forest and large grassy meadows. For the best views of a beaver dam, cross the bridge and travel the loop in a counterclockwise direction. Benches for resting or wildlife viewing are spaced evenly along the trail.

Back on the main trail, continue your journey through a hardwood forest—big-leaf maple, vine maple, and alder are brilliantly colored each autumn—before crossing back over Woods Creek and returning to the parking area. While this trail is primarily flat, there are four very short sections where the gradient reaches 8 percent.

62
IRON CREEK

Accessibility:	Moderate
Distance:	1.5 mile loop
Gradient:	Generally flat, to 5%
Surface:	Gravel
When to go:	March–November
Parking:	Designated
Restrooms:	Yes
Information:	USFS Randle District, (360) 497-7565

There's something about the sight and sound of water gurgling over rocks and dropping into glistening pools that comforts the human soul. That type of sensory experience is found along the first half of this trail as it follows the beautiful Cispus River. To ensure that trail users have the opportunity to thoroughly experience and enjoy the beauty of the river and its environs, the trail is punctuated

The Cispus River from the Iron Creek Camp trail

with occasional benches and turnouts, providing places for rest and contemplation. In addition to enjoying the water, be sure to look for evidence of an old railroad trestle over the riverbed.

That's just the first half. As the trail leaves the river on the northwest corner of the loop, signs identify 600-year-old Douglas firs looming alongside the route. The trees are about 8 feet in diameter and upwards of 280 feet tall. The forest is mostly Douglas fir and western red cedar, but there is a handful of hardwoods scattered around, providing a pleasant sense of diversity.

From Packwood, follow US Highway 12 west to Randle, and at the stoplight turn south on State Route 131. This highway becomes Forest Service Road 23/25. Cross the bridge just after town, and at the next fork in the road, stay right. Follow Road 25 to the Iron Creek Camp area, about 11 miles from the road fork. The campground has four loop camping areas. The trail makes a complete loop around the camping areas.

At the picnic area (near the entrance at the junction of Roads 25 and 76) is a 0.3 mile-long, signed old-growth interpretive loop that intersects the main loop trail. The interpretive signs offer insight into the old-growth ecosystem and the root disease that has affected the area. As the loop trail approaches the picnic area, take care not to be confused by the intersecting campground trails.

63
YELLOW JACKET PONDS

Accessibility: Moderate
Distance: 0.25 mile loop
Gradient: To 3%
Surface: Gravel
When to go: All year
Parking: Designated
Restrooms: Yes
Information: USFS Randle District, (360) 497-7565

The trail loops around the north pond with extensions on either side of the south pond, providing plenty of opportunities to enjoy the scenery and study the aquatic ecosystems. But the real lure here is the fishing.

The always-hungry rainbow trout offer an irresistible pull on the angler in us all. With several accessible fishing piers extending out onto the pond, as well as fishing pads of compacted gravel, this is an angler's dream. Try casting spinners or salmon eggs, unless you're a purist, in which case you will want to tie on a nymph and fly-cast along the shoreline.

From Packwood, follow US Highway 12 west to Randle, and at the stoplight turn south on State Route 131. This highway becomes Forest Service Road 23/25. At the next fork, bear left (Road 23) and

Fishing piers at Yellow Jacket Ponds (Photo: USFS, Gifford Pinchot National Forest)

drive 8 miles to Road 28 (signed Cispus Learning Center). Turn right, and after 0.9 mile, Yellow Jacket Ponds is on the right.

At this site all picnic tables are accessible, and most are on compacted gravel pads.

64   Ⓜ ✿ ☀ ❀ ❄

CISPUS BRAILLE TRAIL

Accessibility: Moderate
Distance: 0.9 mile loop
Gradient: Generally flat, to 10%
Surface: Dirt
When to go: All year
Parking: Designated, at Education Building
Restrooms: No
Information: USFS Randle District, (360) 497-7565

With all the attention that ancient forests receive, it is easy to overlook some of the equally splendid young forests that grace the Northwest. This trail, though, leads through an area, once ravaged by a pair of forest fires, that now hosts a vibrant second-growth stand of forest. This example of natural forest rebirth and renewal, coupled with a well-planned and well-constructed trail, makes this an excellent interpretive walk, complete with stations indicated by Braille markings. Trail guides are available at the Cispus Learning Center office.

From Packwood, follow US Highway 12 west to Randle, and at the stoplight turn south on State Route 131. At the next fork in the road, stay left on Road 23. Continue on until you come to Road 28. Turn right on Road 28 and drive for 1.3 miles, then bear right on Road 76. After 0.7 mile, turn right into the Cispus Learning Center. Take the first right after the office. There is a parking area on the left, past the Education Building and before Elderberry Lodge.

Across from the parking area, the trail enters the forest. In about 200 feet the trail crosses Road 76, where the official beginning of the trail is marked by a Lions Club sign. The first 0.13 mile is narrow, but after that the trail opens up to about 48 inches in width.

To assist the visually impaired, the right side of the trail is bounded by a system of stakes set about 15 feet apart with a rope strung between. Various interpretive stations are marked by small Braille-numbered buttons attached to the rope.

65 🄳 ☀🌿
QUARTZ CREEK BIG TREES

Accessibility:	Difficult
Distance:	0.5 mile loop
Gradient:	To 12%
Surface:	Gravel
When to go:	June–October
Parking:	Usable
Restrooms:	Yes
Information:	USFS Randle District, (360) 497-7565

Throughout the world, Washington is known as home to some of the last remnants of ancient forests. This trail celebrates the magnificent old trees that are the life of those forests. It meanders through old-growth groves of Douglas fir, hemlock, Pacific silver fir, western red cedar, and some hardwoods, but the real highlights of the trail are the several truly giant Douglas firs scattered along the route.

From Packwood, follow US Highway 12 west to Randle, and at the stoplight turn south on State Route 131. This highway becomes Forest Service Road 23/25. Cross the bridge just after town, and at the next fork stay right (Road 25) until you reach an intersection with Road 26. Take Road 26 a little over 8 miles, then turn right on Road 2608. After 1.3 miles you arrive at the parking area.

Because the parking area is above the trailhead and requires a steep descent in loose gravel to the trailhead kiosk, it may be necessary to have a driver shuttle trail users down to the kiosk.

Trail guides are available at the kiosk. While the trail itself is generally under a 5 percent grade, there are short sections up to 12 percent. A short section of the route is on boardwalk with approximately a 10 percent incline. The trail makes a loop and rejoins the parking area above the kiosk nearer to the parking area.

This site features barrier-free campsites, picnic tables, water faucets, and charcoal grills.

66
META LAKE

Accessibility:	Easy
Distance:	0.5 mile round trip
Gradient:	To 5%
Surface:	Pavement
When to go:	June–November
Parking:	Designated
Restrooms:	No
Information:	Mount St. Helens National Volcanic Monument, (360) 247-5473

Despite the incredible amount of destruction wrought by the May 18, 1980, eruption of Mount St. Helens, not all life on the flanks of the volcano was extinguished. This trail focuses on the survivors of that fiery blast.

From Packwood, follow US Highway 12 west to Randle, and at the stoplight turn south on State Route 131. This highway becomes Forest Service Road 23/25. Cross the bridge just outside of town, and at the next fork stay right (Road 25). Continue to milepost 19 and the intersection with Road 99. Turn right on Road 99, and drive to the intersection with Road 26. The trailhead is just beyond the intersection.

Winding through a forest of small alpine and noble firs, the survivors are all around. These 8- to 15-foot-tall trees were shielded from the intense heat of the eruption by a protective layer of heavy snow. The lake environment, too, was protected under a layer of ice and snow, and the eastern brook trout, numerous amphibian species, and aquatic plants that thrive in Meta Lake all owe their continued existence to a heavy winter snowpack.

The survivors, though, were in the minority. Taller trees that towered above the snow were flattened, and larger animals were killed—or they fled before the eruption occurred. Illustrating that not even modern conveniences can outrun the forces of nature, a miner's car lies devastated near the trailhead.

Today the devastation of the region is fading as plants and animals return. The trail linking the wrecked automobile to Meta Lake passes through lush, green marsh grass, fed by the waters of a new, still-occupied beaver dam. If you miss seeing the animal known as "nature's engineer" on the way in toward the lake, keep an eye out on your return trip, since to return to the parking area, you must turn around and travel the same trail.

67
MOUNT ST. HELENS VISITOR CENTER

Accessibility:	Difficult
Distance:	0.25 mile round trip
Gradient:	From 10% to 12%
Surface:	Pavement and gravel
When to go:	All year
Parking:	Designated
Restrooms:	Yes
Information:	Mount St. Helens National Volcanic Monument, (360) 247-5473

This trail explores a lake caught in a mid-life crisis. While it is still a big, beautiful lake in full splendor, Silver Lake is well into the transformation process that will eventually turn the lake into a meadow. Already, the edges of the lake have been claimed by grasses that hold sediment and decaying matter. Slowly, these materials settle to the bottom, making the edges of the lake shallower and shallower until the shoreline starts to creep in toward the middle of the lake. Silver Lake has a long life to live as a lake, but it is interesting to watch the transformation take place.

From Seattle, drive south on Interstate 5 to exit 49. Take this exit and continue east on State Route 504 for 5 miles to the visitor center. The center is on the right side of the road, across from Seaquest State Park.

From the parking area, go toward the visitor center. The trailhead is to your left, just before you reach the building's door. The trail descends in an S-curve of pavement and tile. At the first landing are two telescopes for viewing Mount St. Helens over Silver Lake. One of the scopes is accessible. Continuing down steeply, the trail makes another curve, which is also pitched outward. As the trail levels off, it reaches a fork.

The right fork continues on pavement and goes around the building, ending at a flight of stairs. From this fork there are views of the wetlands—areas in the process of being reclaimed as dry land—and waterfowl on Silver Lake. The left fork, which is the main trail, turns to gravel and follows the lakeshore for almost 0.13 mile before ending. The views of the lake and its inhabitants are excellent. At the fork are several trees honeycombed by woodpecker holes.

The Forest Service hopes to lengthen the trail in 1996 by building a boardwalk through the wetlands and connecting the two forks of the trail. At that time the S-curves will be removed and the gradient reduced, making the trail far more accessible.

68
COLDWATER LAKE

Accessibility:	Easy
Distance:	0.13 mile, one way
Gradient:	Flat
Surface:	Asphalt and boardwalk
When to go:	May–October
Parking:	Designated
Restrooms:	Yes
Information:	Mount St. Helens National Volcanic Monument, (360) 274-2100

Nature has a way of maintaining a balance. The 1980 eruption of Mount St. Helens, for example, destroyed the beautiful Spirit Lake but created the brand-new Coldwater Lake.

Coldwater Lake

Surrounded by the devastation wrought by the eruption, Coldwater Lake is a crystal-blue gem that teems with life. Bird and fish thrive there, living off the aquatic plants and insects that colonized the new lake shortly after it was created.

The trail explores the shore of this new lake and the life it supports. Beginning at a rest area equipped with a bench and well-designed interpretive signs, the trail leads out along the lakeshore and skirts a large volcanic debris pile on the left. Spaced out at various intervals, three small piers branch off the trail and jut out into the lake, providing opportunities to rest and enjoy the beauty of the water. Benches are provided on all the piers.

The main trail forks at the end of the asphalt. The barrier-free trail continues to the right along a wide boardwalk, which circles a small islet before ending at a bench and interpretive signs detailing the dynamic changes that took place in Spirit, Silver, Coldwater, and Castle lakes.

Those who are up for a very strenuous physical challenge may make a loop trip out of this hike by staying left at the fork (instead of following the boardwalk to the right). This alternative is very steep, and only the strongest individuals or most powerful motorized chairs can make it.

From Olympia, follow Interstate 5 south, take exit 49 to State Route 504, and continue east to the Coldwater Ridge Visitor Center at milepost 43. There are signs directing you to Coldwater Lake at the bottom of the ridge. Just before the lake, there is a fork. Take the right fork into a small picnic area. There are three accessible parking spaces plus one for a recreational vehicle.

69

D ☘ ☀ ☙

COLDWATER RIDGE

Accessibility: Difficult
Distance: 0.3 mile
Gradient: Flat, with short 8% descent
Surface: Asphalt
When to go: May–October
Parking: Designated
Restrooms: Yes
Information: USFS Mount St. Helens, (360) 274-2100

This trail gives you a wonderful opportunity to see firsthand both the devastation caused by the May 1980 eruption of Mount St. Helens and the slow rebirth of life in the area. Excellent interpretive stations along the route explain how the ash-laden, 670 miles-per-hour wind from the blast leveled the area. The displays also offer explanations of how some plants and animals were sheltered from the blast and the way new plants and animals have begun to colonize and reclaim the devastated areas.

If the stark scenery isn't evidence enough of the volcano's power, the trail provides a straight-on look into the gaping maw of the mountain. The huge crater opens toward the visitor center, and from the trail visitors can look directly in and see the lava dome deep within the huge hole.

The trail, leading counterclockwise, begins with a descending

Mount St. Helens from the Coldwater Ridge trail

S turn that represents the steepest section of the trail. Once down the curves, the rest of the trail is relatively flat. Several benches are spaced around the loop to provide ample opportunity for visitors to rest and reflect on the power of nature. In the early season there are brilliant displays of wildflowers throughout the valley, including lupine, penstemons, fireweed, and wild strawberries.

From Olympia, follow Interstate 5 south, take exit 49 to State Route 504, and continue east to the Coldwater Ridge Visitor Center at milepost 43. From the parking area, the trailhead is found by turning right on the sidewalk next to the visitor center and proceeding a few hundred feet to the trail.

After exploring the loop trail, don't forget to stop in at the visitor center, which features excellent interactive displays.

70
TRAIL OF TWO FORESTS

Accessibility: Easy
Distance: 0.25 mile loop
Gradient: From 5% to 8%
Surface: Boardwalk
When to go: April–November
Parking: Designated
Restrooms: Yes
Information: Mount St. Helens National Volcanic Monument, (360) 247-5473

A living forest and a lava-encased ancient forest account for this trail's name.

Today's Douglas fir and western red cedar grow along the bed

Trail of Two Forests

of a 2,000-year-old lava river that flowed over this area during one of the formative eruptions of Mount St. Helens. The river spilled down the flanks of the volcano two millennia ago, and left its mark in basaltic lava formations. Huge ancient-growth trees were engulfed in that fiery flood and consumed by heat and fire, leaving behind mysterious hollow casts of the trees, called tree molds.

A 6-foot-wide boardwalk with varying grades of 5 to 8 percent perches atop the ancient lava river. The scenic loop allows you to discover for yourself the horizontal and vertical molds of those ancient trees, and there are several opportunities to actually climb down into connecting lava molds. Bring a flashlight for exploration if you or your companions can navigate a ladder and crawl on hands and knees. The tubes are great fun!

From Vancouver, follow Interstate 5 north to the Woodland exit. Continue on State Route 503 east through Woodland and Cougar. Just past Cougar Camp, turn north on Forest Service Road 83. After several miles, turn left on Road 8303 (signs indicate this road leads to the Ape Cave). The trailhead is on the left, less than 1 mile after the junction.

71
LAVA CANYON

Accessibility:	Difficult
Distance:	0.5 mile round trip
Gradient:	First part 5%, last 100 yards to 18%
Surface:	Pavement
When to go:	May–October
Parking:	Designated
Restrooms:	Yes
Information:	Mount St. Helens National Volcanic Monument, (360) 247-5473

The May 1980 eruption of Mount St. Helens scoured several centuries worth of debris out of this ancient lava canyon. The chasm was formed long before the first massive eruption of Mount St. Helens more than 3,500 years ago. The eruptions in the intervening years filled the canyon with mud and debris, and it wasn't until 1980 that the canyon was cleaned out once more.

The first portion of the trail leads to a turnout with a lookout area. Interpretive signs and benches line the railings, and in the distance the Muddy River runs through the newly revealed canyon. Looping though a hairpin turn, the trail descends closer to the canyon's edge. A series of winding 8 to 12 percent grades (and one short 20 percent slope) make this trail quite challenging.

At times you can catch a glimpse of the river rushing through the lava cradle. The trail ends at another lookout point with interpretive signs explaining the drama that took place here only a short time ago. Follow the trail as it twists above the timberline, among the alder and lupine, and sense nature's power.

From Vancouver, follow Interstate 5 north to the Woodland exit. Continue on State Route 503 east through Woodland and Cougar. Turn north onto Forest Service Road 83 and follow it to the Lahar Viewpoint/Lava Canyon trailhead.

72
CURLY CREEK FALLS

Accessibility: Moderate
Distance: 0.2 mile round trip
Gradient: To 5%
Surface: Gravel
When to go: April–November
Parking: Usable (loose gravel may require assistance)
Restrooms: Yes
Information: Mount St. Helens National Volcanic Monument, (360) 247-5473

Following a gentle slope above the Lewis River, this trail offers viewing at not one but two waterfalls. The 5-foot-wide trail departs from a thickly graveled parking area and winds along a 6 to 8 percent grade through timber up to the first viewpoint. Here you have an obstructed view across the river to the emerald green waters of Curly Falls. The trail continues a little farther to the Miller Creek Falls lookout, where you briefly encounter steeper grades, up to 25 percent. The Miller Falls outlook marks the end of the trail, but it does so spectacularly, with a glimpse of Miller Creek plunging over lava cliffs into the pools of the Lewis River far below.

During fishing season, watch the river on the return trip; you may see anglers casting for big trout and steelhead.

From Vancouver, follow Interstate 5 north to the Woodland exit. Continue on State Route 503 east through Woodland and Cougar and into the Gifford Pinchot National Forest. Just past the Pine Creek Information Center, turn right onto Forest Service Road 90. Follow Road 90 up the Lewis River to Road 9039. Turn left on Road 9039, cross the bridge, and park at the Curly Creek Falls Viewpoint.

73
BIG CREEK FALLS

Accessibility:	Moderate to difficult
Distance:	0.1 mile loop
Gradient:	From 5% to 11%
Surface:	Gravel and dirt
When to go:	May–October
Parking:	Designated
Restrooms:	No
Information:	Mount St. Helens National Volcanic Monument, (360) 247-5473

The view of the falls is spectacular, but so is the experience of getting there. This loop trail wanders through beautiful Douglas firs, pausing for interpretive signs that include poems and excerpts from essays written about the area.

From Vancouver, follow Interstate 5 north to the Woodland exit. Continue on State Route 503 east through Woodland and Cougar and into the Gifford Pinchot National Forest. Just past the Pine Creek Information Center, turn right onto Forest Service Road 90. Follow Road 90 to the trailhead, past Forest Service Road 9039.

The trail maintains an average 6 percent grade, but a few areas climb to as much as 11 percent. Beginning the trail in a counter-clockwise direction makes your arrival at the falls a surprise. Before reaching the outlook you hear the pounding of water, and before you realize it the falls seem to burst out of nowhere, falling into a beautiful round basin carved perfectly from the lava-scape.

The falls are particularly spectacular during the late spring and early summer when the river is swollen with the runoff from the melting snows.

74

M 🌷 ☀ 🌿

LEWIS RIVER
LOWER FALLS VIEWPOINT

Accessibility: Moderate
Distance: 0.2 mile round trip
Gradient: First part to 6%, last part to 13%
Surface: Gravel
When to go: April–November
Parking: Designated
Restrooms: Yes
Information: Mount St. Helens National Volcanic Monument, (360) 247-5473

Following a beautiful river to crashing waterfalls, this trail has it all—and it is accessible to all.

The Lower Falls Recreation Area is an excellent example of accessibility to the outdoors. The area boasts 43 barrier-free campsites with accessible picnic tables. The area also offers the Lower Falls Trail, which begins in the day-use parking area and continues all the way to the Lewis River Lower Falls. The first 300 feet of trail have a grade of 6 percent, then it levels off to the end of the trail. Three lookout areas are scattered along the route; each has handrails and benches along with spectacular views of the open, sunny river. Looking down from the viewpoint above the falls, try to make out the lava casts deep in the river's bottom, reminders of the volcanic nature of this region.

The last 200 feet of the trail are on a boardwalk and head down to the river's edge, with a grade of 11 to 13 percent. By the time the trail comes to the riverbank, the water is serene, and you are far enough above the falls to be out of earshot of the crashing water. In this riverside area is an amphitheater where summer campers can occasionally enjoy musical and theatrical performances.

From Vancouver, follow Interstate 5 north to the Woodland exit. Continue on State Route 503 east through Woodland and Cougar

Lewis River Lower Falls

and into the Gifford Pinchot National Forest. Just past the Pine Creek Information Center, turn right onto Forest Service Road 90. Follow Road 90 to the trailhead.

75

PEELED CEDAR

Ⓜ 🌷 ☀ 🌿

Accessibility: Moderate
Distance: 0.12 mile loop
Gradient: To 5%
Surface: Gravel
When to go: May–October
Parking: Designated
Restrooms: No
Information: USFS Mount Adams District, (509) 395-2501

Scenic splendor and historical wonders abound on this trail. Looping through a Douglas fir forest, the trail and surrounding area provide great views of Mount Adams, alpine meadows, and a diversity of flora. In the spring and early summer, the meadows are ablaze with brilliantly colored wildflowers. Autumn visitors will be pleasantly surprised by the number of larches—one of the few members of the conifer family that turn yellow and drop their needles every fall—scattered throughout the area. The bright gold autumn larches provide a refreshing contrast to the surrounding dark green forest.

From Vancouver, follow State Route 14 east along the Columbia River to the junction with State Route 141. Turn north onto Route 141 and continue to Trout Lake. Take Forest Service Road 88 north out of town, drive 12.7 miles to the Historic Site marker, and turn left at the sign into a parking area.

As the trail begins, it loops through a mostly Douglas fir grove. Traveling counterclockwise, you will find the peeled cedars at the first interpretive sign. These trees were a primary resource for the region's native Americans. The cedar's bark was one of the most important commodities in their daily lives. The strong, fibrous inner bark was stripped from old-growth cedars and used in a variety

Cedars from which the bark has been peeled (Photo: Greg Ball)

of tasks. Strips were woven into bags and baskets, floor mats, sails for canoes (which were in turn usually made from dug-out cedar logs—after the bark had been stripped), and even clothing.

The grove of old-growth cedars along this trail shows long-healed scars where, centuries ago, native Americans gathered the bark. Interpretive signage explains the ancient bark collection procedure and the importance of this area to the local tribes.

EASTERN WASHINGTON

76
SPOKANE RIVER CENTENNIAL TRAIL

Accessibility: Easy
Distance: 40 miles round trip (various access/exit points)
Gradient: To 8%
Surface: Pavement
When to go: All year (except when snow- and ice-covered)
Parking: Usable (reserved spaces planned)
Restrooms: Yes (but few and far between; more planned)
Information: Spokane County Parks and Recreation, (509) 456-4730

Thousands of years ago an ice dam broke across the Pend Oreille River Gorge. A spectacular flood, at times thousands of feet deep, swept through the Inland Empire and created the Spokane River as we know it.

In 1986 a handful of citizens unveiled a plan for the Spokane River Centennial Trail. This multi-use pathway will eventually follow the river for 39 miles in the state of Washington and 21 miles in the state of Idaho. Several miles of trail in the city of Spokane have been completed. There are multiple access points all along the Spokane River.

The Spokane River Centennial Trail begins near the old Spokane House fur trading post, stretching southward through Riverside State Park. It continues to thread its way along until both river and trail meet the mighty falls in downtown Spokane's famous Riverfront Park. From here, when complete, it will wind eastward through the Spokane Valley to the state line.

There are a number of historic landmarks and points of interest along the trail's route, from the Long Lake petroglyphs to the site of Colonel Wright's brutal action in the war against the native tribes, aptly and vividly named Horse Slaughter Island Camp. No motorized vehicles, except wheelchairs, are allowed on the path.

A somewhat accessible restroom is currently located at the Walk in the Wild Zoo trail access point (located at Euclid Street, just east

The Pend Oreille River from Pioneer Park (Photo: Mary Masterson)

153

Pedestrian bridge on the Spokane River Centennial Trail (Photo: Marge and Ted Mueller)

of Pines). New accessible restrooms are slated to be installed before 1996 at Upriver Drive just west of Plantes Ferry Park.

Most of the Centennial Trail will be 12 feet wide and paved. It will be supported by fourteen trailheads, each equipped with parking facilities, power, water, picnic tables, hitching posts, restrooms, directories, and river access.

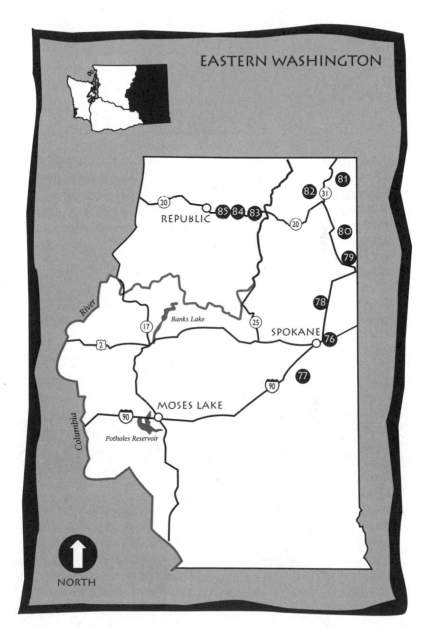

EASTERN WASHINGTON

REPUBLIC

81
82 31
80
79
78
85 84 83
20
20
25
River
Banks Lake
17
2
SPOKANE
76
Columbia
90
77
MOSES LAKE
90
Potholes Reservoir

NORTH

77

BLACKHORSE LAKE BOARDWALK, TURNBULL NATIONAL WILDLIFE REFUGE

Accessibility: Easy
Distance: 0.5 mile loop
Gradient: Flat
Surface: Boardwalk
When to go: All year (except when snow-covered)
Parking: Designated
Restrooms: Yes
Information: Turnbull National Wildlife Refuge, (509) 235-4723

Like most wildlife refuges, Turnbull is best visited early in the morning or at dusk. At these times visitors are treated to a wild symphony,

Viewing platform in the Turnbull National Wildlife Refuge
(Photo: Mary Masterson)

since birds and animals are active and audible. During the migration seasons (from November through January birds head south; from May through July they head back north), more than 200 species of birds have been sighted, and the total bird population around the lake can reach 50,000 in the fall.

In addition to the visiting birds, the resident population of mammals includes elk, white-tailed and mule deer, coyotes, beavers, porcupines, badgers, muskrats, and skunks.

From Spokane, follow Interstate 90 to exit 270 at Cheney/Four Lakes, and follow State Route 904 south to Cheney, where the highway becomes First Street. At the K Street intersection, turn south and continue (this becomes Cheney Plaza Road) 5.5 miles to the entrance to the Turnbull National Wildlife Refuge. Follow the road as it loops around to the west side of the lake and the trailhead parking area.

The wide boardwalk explores the lakeshore before crossing a narrow neck of water to a secluded island frequented by feeding ducks, geese, and beavers.

Springtime visitors will enjoy the brilliant meadows painted all colors of the rainbow with the blooms of buttercups, grass widows, yellow bells, larkspur, wild iris, lupine, and paintbrush.

78

BEAR LAKE

Accessibility:	Easy
Distance:	1.4 mile loop
Gradient:	Generally flat
Surface:	Pavement
When to go:	June–September, closed Monday
Parking:	Designated
Restrooms:	Yes
Information:	Spokane County Parks, (509) 996-2266

Circling the lake, this park trail offers a chance to study the animals of a marshy wetland, to fish for fat rainbow and golden trout, and to simply enjoy an outing along the shore of a beautiful upland lake.

From Spokane, drive approximately 17 miles north on State Route 2 (the Newport Highway). The park is 0.7 mile north of Chattaroy, on the west side of the highway, and the park entrance sign is visible from Route 2.

The paved trail completely encircles the lake, with the best trailhead found on the west side of the lake, where the road ends in a large parking area. The trail starts here, in a large grassy park, then passes along the marshy, northern side of the lake, with its tall reeds and lily pads. Along the east side, accessible platforms extend into the lake for those interested in fishing or just admiring the beauty of the water. The trail again passes a wetland ecosystem on the south bank and completes the loop among tall pines.

79
PIONEER PARK

Accessibility:	Difficult
Distance:	0.3 mile loop
Gradient:	Generally flat, to 10%
Surface:	Unpacked gravel and boardwalk
When to go:	May–October
Parking:	Designated
Restrooms:	Yes
Information:	USFS Newport District, (509) 447-3129

The pioneers behind this trail established their settlement nearly 4,000 years ago. Long before Europeans set foot on this continent, the Kalispell Indians were living and working on the current trail site. Evidence of their presence is still visible. In fact, one of the highlights of this unique site is a camas oven where the Kalispells once cooked camas root. This is the oldest and largest native American food processing site in the Pacific Northwest. The oven has been excavated and is visible beneath a Plexiglas cover.

Native Americans throughout the region battled for the right to harvest the camas meadows. They would dig up the small camas bulbs and roast them in rock ovens like the one found here. The bulbs, when properly cooked, taste like sweet potatoes.

Golden and bald eagles are common in the area and are often seen soaring over the Camas Plains and the river, looking for their next meal, usually a fat rainbow trout or a plump rabbit.

To make sure visitors fully appreciate the trail experience, signage has been placed on twelve interpretive stations, explaining all the uses of the site. The sign text is written in both English and the Kalispell language.

From Newport, follow State Route 2 over the Pend Oreille River. Turn left (north) immediately after crossing the bridge, and drive 2.3 miles on Forest Service Road 9305 to the entrance of the Pioneer Park Campground.

This fine interpretive trail guarantees a great visit, especially from the historical perspective. The trail makes a loop on some low ridges above the river, and the boardwalk section offers great views. The campground closes after Labor Day and is gated at the entrance.

Pioneer Park trail near the Pend Oreille River (Photo: Mary Masterson)

80
BROWNS LAKE

Accessibility: Difficult
Distance: 0.25 mile one way
Gradient: Generally flat
Surface: Gravel
When to go: May–October
Parking: Usable
Restrooms: No
Information: USFS Newport District, (509) 447-3129

The lucky few will hit this trail just as the cutthroat trout are spawning in the spring. From a boardwalk overlook, the red-sided fish are

Viewing platform at Browns Lake (Photo: USFS, Newport Ranger District)

easily visible thrashing about the spawning beds in a stream feeding into the lake. Fish ladders have been added to the stream to help the fish make it to the spawning grounds, and these add to the trail experience: during the spawn, you may catch a glimpse of the passionate fish leaping up the ladder.

From the viewing pad, the trail extends to a grove of ancient cedars and firs.

From Newport, follow State Route 20 north to Usk. Turn west on Kings Lake Road (Forest Service Road 3389) and cross the Pend Oreille River. Continue on for 6.2 miles to a junction with Road 5030. Bear left on Road 5030 and follow it to Browns Lake Campground. The trail actually starts 1 mile north of the campground on the continuation of Road 5030. This road is not maintained for passenger vehicles.

Tucked away in the remote northeastern corner of the state, Browns Lake is hidden in a dark and steep valley system. Getting there is half the fun, as the road weaves through deep, dark forests of ancient cedar, Douglas fir, and larch.

81
MILL POND

Accessibility: Moderate
Distance: 0.5 mile loop
Gradient: Generally flat
Surface: Gravel, grass, and dirt patches
When to go: May–November
Parking: Designated
Restrooms: Yes
Information: USFS Sullivan Lake District, (509) 446-2681

At the turn of the century Lewis Larsen discovered a mountain of limestone on the east side of the Pend Oreille River, above Metaline Falls. To exploit this resource he needed both power and the railroad, located at Newport, 60 miles to the south. He managed to put together one package for bringing up the railroad and building a

Old log cabin near Mill Pond (Photo: Greg Ball)

power-generating plant. To power the plant, a long flume was built to a generator mill and, eventually, to a mill pond. The pond level was later raised by building a high earthen levee around it. This trail follows that structure.

From Colville, follow State Route 20 east to the junction with State Route 31 at Tiger. Turn north onto Route 31 and continue north through Metaline Falls. Turn east on Sullivan Lake Road. Drive 3.2 miles to the entrance of the parking area on the left side of the road.

After leaving the parking area, the trail immediately crosses a spectacular bridge over the outlet of the mill pond. Views of the deep river gorge, on the downstream side of the bridge, are awesome. Leaving the bridge, the trail follows the lakeshore for a short distance before beginning the loop. For the best views, do the loop clockwise. Several interpretive signs explain the history of the area. The flume keeper's cabin still remains with some other outbuildings, as do remnants of the old flume. The views of surrounding countryside are excellent, and the autumn colors make this spot a wonderful choice for a late-season trip.

82
BIG MEADOW LAKE

Ⓜ 🌷☀🌿

Accessibility: Moderate
Distance: 0.3 mile loop
Gradient: Flat
Surface: Gravel
When to go: May–October
Parking: Designated
Restrooms: Yes
Information: USFS Colville District, (509) 684-4557

This spectacular trail overlooks a sparkling lake in a high, dry, ponderosa pine valley. As you work your way up to the overlook, you loop past wetland. For wildlife lovers, a viewing area offers great views of the wetland and all its occupants—from mice to mule deer, not to mention the barrage of birds. The lake overlook sports a three-story viewing tower, but it isn't accessible.

Though the scenery is impressive, sadly, the trail itself isn't too grand. It is necessary to cross the loose, wheel-grabbing gravel of the campground road to reach the trailhead, and at the time of our visit the trail needed maintenance; grass was growing through the gravel, and large gopher mounds pockmarked the route. At the point where the loop returns to the trailhead, the trail had not been completed at the time of our visit, forcing the user to travel 250 feet on the road to get back to the start.

From Colville, follow State Route 20 east to the junction with State Route 31 at Tiger. Turn north onto Route 31 and continue on to Ione. In the town, go west on Houghton Street and drive 0.4 mile to Greenhouse Road. Turn left on Greenhouse and drive 0.1 mile before turning right on Smackout Pass Road. The pavement ends 1.2 miles from Ione. After 2.5 miles on Smackout Pass Road, turn left on County Road 2695 (the sign is riddled with bullet holes). After 5.3 miles, enter the Big Meadow Recreation Area. Park in the first parking area after crossing the outlet of the lake.

After tiring of the trail, visitors may venture farther along the campground road to a fishing pier on the lake. The pier has been made accessible by a ramp leading down from the road, but the dock's railings may present an obstacle to fishing, as no areas have been cut down to a wheelchair user's height.

83
LOG FLUME

Accessibility:	Moderate
Distance:	0.5 mile loop
Gradient:	Generally flat, to 8%
Surface:	Gravel and pavement
When to go:	May–October
Parking:	Designated
Restrooms:	Yes
Information:	USFS Kettle Falls District, (509) 738-6111

Take a hike through time on this trail, back a century or more to a time when loggers used saws powered by muscle and sweat. Back to a time before logging trucks and diesel-powered winches. Back to a time when the only way to get logs off a mountain was to shoot them down flumes—long, wooden, slide-like chutes, sometimes filled with water, that carried the logs over stumps and obstacles on the way down the mountainside.

This trail offers an up-close look at some of the last flumes still standing in Washington. Interpretive signs dot the route, offering clear explanations of how the loggers used the flumes—with examples of wet and dry flumes in evidence—to bring the logs to the mills.

From Republic, follow State Route 20 east to Sherman Pass. Continue east from the pass until you reach the trailhead, just past Canyon Creek Campground at milepost 335. The trailhead is well marked with an interpretive kiosk.

As it passes the flumes, the trail wanders through a lodgepole forest, the remains of the 1929 Dollar Fire.

Midway along the route, a side trail drops down a hill. This trail is not accessible, as it is narrow and very steep (with more than a

20 percent grade). If you stay on the main trail, however, you won't miss a thing. The hazardous spur passes the remnants of the old wet flume, which is easily seen from the main trail as well.

Just past this junction, the main (safe!) trail eventually crosses a bridge over the old railroad cut and returns to the parking area.

84
CANYON CREEK

Accessibility:	Moderate
Distance:	2 miles round trip
Gradient:	Generally flat, short grades to 8%
Surface:	Gravel
When to go:	May–October
Parking:	Designated
Restrooms:	Yes
Information:	USFS Kettle Falls District, (509) 738-6111

With multiple opportunities to stop and peer down on the tumbling water of Sherman Creek, this is a water lover's trail.

As you wander through a modest lodgepole pine forest—the offspring of an older forest destroyed by the 1929 Dollar Fire—the trail repeatedly returns to the creek. First a bridge crosses the waterway, and then it parallels the creek. Two turnouts feature platforms over the water, perfect places for those seeking rest and thoughtful reflection. Between the turnouts, there are several benches along the trail for those who want more frequent breaks (this is especially nice on the return, uphill trip).

From Republic, follow State Route 20 east to Sherman Pass. Continue east from the pass until you reach the trailhead, in Canyon Creek Campground at milepost 334. The trailhead is at the entrance to the campground loop.

The generally flat trail banks slightly downhill from Canyon Creek Campground until it reaches the Log Flume interpretive area. The return trip is obviously uphill. This trip can be combined with the Log Flume Trail. If transportation can be arranged, it makes a

Meadow near Canyon Creek (Photo: Greg Ball)

nice downhill (or from the Log Flume, a challenging uphill) one-way trip. It can be hot and dry on the east side of the mountains, so bring plenty to drink.

As you start down the hill near the campground, notice that several trees show the vertical scratches of visiting black bears. The chance that you will see one of the bruins is slight, but the scratches show that they still occasionally visit these parts.

Two accessible fishing platforms are slated for completion by the time this guide goes to press.

85
SHERMAN PASS

M ☙ ☀ ⚘

Accessibility: Moderate
Distance: 0.25 mile round trip
Gradient: Flat, with short grades to 8%
Surface: Gravel
When to go: May–October
Parking: Designated
Restrooms: Yes
Information: USFS Republic District, (509) 775-3305

This could easily be called a trail of two fires. As the trail meanders over one of the highest passes in the state, the scenery changes dramatically. On the west side of the pass, the charred remains of a forest are all that was left after fire swept through 20,000 acres of Douglas fir and cedar. Note that although the area was ravaged by an inferno less than a decade before, the land is rich with life. Pileated woodpeckers jackhammer into the standing stumps; deer wander through the burn site, feeding on the rich ground cover; hawks and the occasional eagle soar overhead, feeding on the rodents that are left unprotected by the loss of a cloaking forest canopy.

As you crest over to the eastern slope of the pass, the legacy of a 1929 fire greets you. Here, only an occasional larch or Douglas fir is visible amid the thick growth of lodgepole pine that now carpets the old burn. Visitors here have a chance to view nature's process of healing the wounds of massive forest fires.

From Republic, follow State Route 20 east to the summit of Sherman Pass. The trailhead is just on the east side of the pass, on the north side of the highway.

APPENDICES

A. TRAILS IN THIS BOOK

* E=easy   M=moderate   D=difficult

Hike # and Name	Accessibility	Distance	When to go	Restrooms	Parking
OLYMPICS					
1 Rialto Beach	E*	0.1 mi	All year	Yes	Designated
2 Pioneer Trail	M	0.25 mi	All year	Yes	Usable
3 Hoh Mini-Loop Nature Trail	E	0.25 mi	June–Oct	Yes	Designated
4 Salmon Cascades	E	0.1 mi	All year	Yes	Designated
5 Barnes Point Nature Trail	M	1 mi	All year	Yes	Designated
6 Marymere Falls	M	0.8 mi	All year	Yes	Designated
7 Madison Falls Trail	E	200 yards	All year	Yes	Designated
8 Hurricane Hill	D	0.5 mi	May–Oct	No	Designated
9 Hurricane Ridge Meadow	D	0.5 mi	May–Oct	Yes	Designated
10 Port Angeles Waterfront Trail	E	10 mi	All year	Yes	Designated
11 Dungeness National Wildlife Refuge	M	0.75 mi	All year	Yes	Designated
12 Railroad Bridge	E	1 mi	All year	No	Usable
13 Seal Rock	D	0.25 mi	All year	Yes	Designated
14 Island Lake	E	1 mi	All year	Yes	Designated
15 Hood Canal Wetlands	E	3.8 mi	All year	Yes	Designated
16 Pete's Creek	D	0.5 mi	April–Oct	Yes	Designated
17 Mima Mounds	E	0.5 mi	All year	Yes	Usable
18 Long Beach Boardwalk	E	0.8 mi	All year	Yes	Designated

Hike # and Name	Accessibility	Distance	When to go	Restrooms	Parking
Olympics cont.					
19 Julia Butler Hansen National Wildlife Refuge	M	4 mi	All year	No	Usable
NORTH CASCADES					
20 Deception Pass Sand Dune Trail	E	0.8 mi	All year	Yes	Usable
21 Padilla Bay	E	5.75 mi	All year	Yes	Designated
22 Picture Lake	E	0.25 mi	July–Oct	No	Designated
23 Austin Pass Picnic Area/Fire and Ice I and II	E to D	0.26 mi	July–Oct	Yes	Designated
24 Artist Ridge and Artist Point	E	0.25 mi	Aug–Oct	Yes	Designated
25 Shadow of the Sentinels	E	0.5 mi	All year	Yes	Designated
26 Sterling Munro	E	110 yards	All year	Yes	Designated
27 Trail of the Cedars	D	0.5 mi	All year	No	Usable
28 Happy Creek	M	0.3 mi	June–Oct	Yes	Designated
29 Rainy Lake	E	1.8 mi	June–Oct	Yes	Designated
30 Washington Pass Overlook	E	0.15 mi	June–Oct	Yes	Designated
31 Lone Fir	E to D	2 mi	June–Oct	Yes	Usable
32 Blackpine Lake	E	0.5 mi	May–Oct	Yes	Usable
33 Sierra Park for the Blind	E	0.25 mi	All year	Yes	Designated
34 Burke-Gilman and Sammamish River Trails	E	54 mi	All year	Yes	Designated
35 Snohomish Centennial Trail	E	14 mi	All year	Yes	Designated
36 Youth on Age	E	0.3 mi	March–Nov	Yes	Usable
37 Iron Goat	M	2.4 mi	March–Nov	Yes	Designated
38 Deception Falls	M	0.4 mi	April–Nov	Yes	Designated

North Cascades cont.

Hike # and Name	Accessibility	Distance	When to go	Restrooms	Parking
39 Confluence and Wenatchee Riverfront Parks	E	10 mi	Feb–Nov	Yes	Designated
40 Washington Park Arboretum	M to D	2 mi	All year	Yes	Designated
41 Coulon Beach	E	3 mi	All year	Yes	Designated
42 Marymoor Interpretive Trail	E	3 mi	All year	Yes	Designated
43 Tradition Lakes	E	0.6 mi	All year	Yes	Usable
44 Snoqualmie River	M	up to 30.2 mi	All Year	No	Usable
45 Creekside Loop at Mount Si	E	500 feet	All Year	Yes	Designated
46 Tinkham Discovery	M	0.5 mi	April–Oct	Yes	Usable
47 Gold Creek Pond	E	1 mi	May–Oct	No	Designated
48 Lake Kachess	M	0.5 mi	April–Oct	Yes	Usable

SOUTH CASCADES

Hike # and Name	Accessibility	Distance	When to go	Restrooms	Parking
49 Woodard Bay Trail	E to D	12 mi	All year	No	Usable
50 Woodard Bay Conservation Area	E	1.2 mi	All year	No	Usable
51 Nisqually National Wildlife Refuge	M	5.5 mi	All year	Yes	Usable
52 West Hylebos Wetlands	E	1 mi	All year	No	Usable
53 Federation forest	M	0.4 mi	May–Aug	Yes	Designated
54 Muir Discovery	E	0.8 mi	April–Nov	Yes	Usable
55 Box Canyon of the Cowlitz	D	0.25 mi	July–Oct	Yes	Designated
56 Paradise Loops	M to D	0.1 mi	July–Nov	Yes	Designated
57 Trail of the Shadows	E to D	0.5 mi	July–Nov	Yes	Designated
58 Clear Lake	E	1.2 mi	May–Oct	Yes	Designated

Hike # and Name	Accessibility	Distance	When to go	Restrooms	Parking
South Cascades cont.					
59 Boulder Cave No. 962A	E	0.75mi	April–Oct	Yes	Designated
60 Yakima Greenway	E	14 mi	All Year	Yes	Designated
61 Woods Creek Watchable Wildlife	M	2.5 mi	March–Nov	Yes	Designated
62 Iron Creek	M	1.5 mi	March–Nov	Yes	Designated
63 Yellow Jacket Ponds	M	0.25mi	All year	Yes	Designated
64 Cispus Braille Trail	M	0.9 mi	All year	No	Designated
65 Quartz Creek Big Trees	D	0.5 mi	June–Oct	Yes	Usable
66 Meta Lake	E	0.5 mi	June–Nov	No	Designated
67 Mount St. Helens Visitor Center	D	0.25 mi	All year	Yes	Designated
68 Coldwater Lake	E	0.13 mi	May–Oct	Yes	Designated
69 Coldwater Ridge	D	0.3 mi	May–Oct	Yes	Designated
70 Trail of Two Forests	E	0.25 mi	April–Nov	Yes	Designated
71 Lava Canyon	D	0.5 mi	May–Oct	Yes	Designated
72 Curly Creek Falls	M	0.2 mi	April–Nov	Yes	Usable
73 Big Creek Falls	M to D	0.1 mi	May–Oct	No	Designated
74 Lewis River Lower Falls Viewpoint	M	0.2 mi	April–Nov	Yes	Designated
75 Peeled Cedar	M	0.12 mi	May–Oct	No	Designated

EASTERN WASHINGTON

Hike # and Name	Accessibility	Distance	When to go	Restrooms	Parking
76 Spokane River Centennial Trail	E	40 mi	All year	Yes	Usable
77 Blackhorse Lake Boardwalk, Turnbull NWR	E	0.5 mi	All year	Yes	Designated
78 Bear Lake	E	1.4 mi	June–Sept	Yes	Designated

Hike # and Name	Accessibility	Distance	When to go	Restrooms	Parking
Eastern Washington cont.					
79 Pioneer Park	D	0.3 mi	May–Oct	Yes	Designated
80 Browns Lake	D	0.25 mi	May–Oct	No	Usable
81 Mill Pond	M	0.5 mi	May–Nov	Yes	Designated
82 Big Meadow Lake	M	0.3 mi	May–Oct	Yes	Designated
83 Log Flume	M	0.5 mi	May–Oct	Yes	Designated
84 Canyon Creek	M	2 mi	May–Oct	Yes	Designated
85 Sherman Pass	M	0.25 mi	May–Oct	Yes	Designated

B. FUTURE TRAILS

Name	Region	Manager	Phone	Date of completion	Distance	Comments
Port Angeles	Olympic	Port Angeles	(360) 457-0411	Undetermined	Unknown	
Port Townsend	Olympic	Jefferson Co	(360) 385-9160	Undetermined	Unknown	New trail
Quinault Loop	Olympic	USFS	(360) 288-2525	Spring 1995	0.5 mile	
Rain Forest Nature	Olympic	USFS	(360) 288-2525	Spring 1995	0.2 mile	Extension of existing trail
Truman Glick	Olympic	Mason Co	(360) 427-9670	Undetermined	Unknown	
Big Four	N Cas	USFS	(360) 436-1155	Summer 1995	1 mile	New trail
Holden Village	N Cas	USFS	(509) 682-2576	Undetermined	Unknown	New trail
Icicle Canyon	N Cas	USFS	(509) 782-1413	Undetermined	Unknown	New trail
Lucerne	N Cas	USFS	(509) 682-2576	Undetermined	Unknown	New trail
Swift Creek	N Cas	USFS	(360) 856-5700	Summer 1997	1 mile	New trail
Hemlock Interpretive	S Cas	USFS	(360) 750-5000	Undetermined	Unknown	New trail
Heart of the Mountain	S Cas	USFS	(360) 247-5473	Undetermined	0.5 mile	In the hummock area beyond Coldwater
Johnston Observatory	S Cas	USFS	(360) 247-5473	Undetermined	Unknown	Closest trail to Mount St. Helens
Mather Highway	S Cas	USFS	(360) 825-6585	Summer 1996	1 mile	Along Highway 410
Silver Lake	S Cas	USFS	(360) 247-5473	Undetermined	Unknown	Extension of existing trail
Takhlakh Lake	S Cas	USFS	(360) 497-7565	Undetermined	Unknown	New trail
Whistle Punk	S Cas	USFS	(509) 427-5645	Undetermined	1.5 miles	New trail
Potholes SP	E Wash	State Parks		Summer 1995	Unknown	Lakeshore trail

INDEX

ABOUT THE
WASHINGTON TRAILS ASSOCIATION

Washington Trails Association (WTA), founded in 1973, is a nonprofit organizaton whose volunteers are dedicated to protecting and expanding Washington's hiking trails through:

- *Education and information programs*
- *Direct involvement in planning and management of public and private lands*
- *Encouragement of cooperative solutions to trail problems statewide*

WTA was formed in response to an alarming trend that began more than forty years ago. Since 1950, Washington state has lost 4,000 miles of hiking trails, while the number of hikers has grown by 800 percent. WTA volunteers are working to protect trails from:

- *careless users*
- *increased motorized use*
- *overdevelopment and overuse*
- *shrinking maintenance budgets*
- *logging*

WTA's projects include:

- *Formation and management of "Trail Crew," an independent, private fund for trail construction and maintenance to supplement shrinking government budgets*
- *A cooperative effort with the U.S. Forest Service and others to provide extensive volunteer trail maintenance in the Mount Baker–Snoqualmie National Forest*
- *Leadership of efforts to convert logging roads to trails*
- *Representation of hikers at hearings, meetings, and conferences on trail proposals and policies*
- *Working with the Forest Service to provide new backcountry trails to relieve pressure on the Alpine Lakes Wilderness Area*
- *A campaign to protect hiking trails from increased motorcycle use*
- *Publication of this book—a guide to barrier-free trails in Washington state*
- *Publication of the monthly magazine* Signpost for Northwest Trails

How can you help improve the hiking trail system in Washington state? Call or write for more information:

Washington Trails Association
1305 Fourth Avenue, Suite 512
Seattle, Washington 98101
(206) 625-1367

ABOUT THE EDITOR

Dan A. Nelson is executive editor of *Signpost for Northwest Trails,* the monthly magazine of the Washington Trails Association. He is also an outdoor recreation columnist for the daily newspaper *The News Tribune* in Tacoma, Washington, and is coauthor of *Pacific Northwest Hiking.* Dan is an avid hiker, backpacker, skier, and snowshoer and has explored and photographed wilderness areas throughout the West. He lives in Puyallup, Washington.

THE MOUNTAINEERS, founded in 1906, is a nonprofit outdoor activity and conservation club, whose mission is "to explore, study, preserve, and enjoy the natural beauty of the outdoors...." Based in Seattle, Washington, the club is now the third-largest such organization in the United States, with 15,000 members and four branches throughout Washington state.

The Mountaineers sponsors both classes and year-round outdoor activities in the Pacific Northwest, which include hiking, mountain climbing, ski-touring, snowshoeing, bicycling, camping, kayaking and canoeing, nature study, sailing, and adventure travel. The club's conservation division supports environmental causes through educational activities, sponsoring legislation, and presenting informational programs. All club activities are led by skilled, experienced volunteers, who are dedicated to promoting safe and responsible enjoyment and preservation of the outdoors.

The Mountaineers Books, an active, nonprofit publishing program of the club, produces guidebooks, instructional texts, historical works, natural history guides, and works on environmental conservation. All books produced by The Mountaineers are aimed at fulfilling the club's mission.

If you would like to participate in these organized outdoor activities or the club's programs, consider a membership in The Mountaineers. For information and an application, write or call The Mountaineers, Club Headquarters, 300 Third Avenue West, Seattle, Washington 98119; (206) 284-6310.

Send or call for our catalog of more than 300 outdoor titles:

The Mountaineers Books
1001 SW Klickitat Way, Suite 102
Seattle, WA 98134
1-800-553-4453